Better Control of Your Destiny by Mastering Qi Men Dun Jia
(奇门遁甲)

Calvin Yap

Copyright © 2014 by Calvin Yap
All rights reserved worldwide.
Second Edition 2017

Some of the information from this book was obtained from the Internet. Acknowledgement is given to the authors and/or creator of Wikipedia, Astro-databank and google in general. Any omission of acknowledgement is unintentional. Please inform the author so that such acknowledgement can be included in the next edition. All other intellectual property rights contained or in relation to this book belongs to Calvin Yap

No part of this book may be copied, used, reproduced or transmitted in any form or by any means, graphic, electronic or mechanical, including photocopying, recording, taping or by any information storage or retrieval system, without the permission in writing from the author.

The authors can be reached at:

Email: Calvin Yap (calvin_yap@yahoo.com)

Website: http://www.fengshui-hacks.com/

Edited by: Jo Lim Yong Chin (jorryn_lim@yahoo.com.sg)

Cover Design by: Jo Lim Yong Chin

Warning and Disclaimer

The information in this book is based on the author's knowledge and personal experience. It is presented for educational purposes to assist the reader in expanding his or her knowledge on Chinese Meta-physics. The techniques and practices are not to be used without any proper training. The author is not responsible in any manner whatsoever for any loses or damages caused or alleged to be caused directly or indirectly from using the information contained in this book.

The author provides both distant learning and on site courses for those who are keen to learn. Please contact the author for arrangement.

Dedication and Acknowledgement

For my family:

> To my wife Lucy & my 2 daughters: Denise & Sherry for their understanding and support.

To my student Jo Lim:

> For her help in editing and her final magic touch.

Contents

Dedication and Acknowledgement *3*

Introduction to Qi Men Dun Jia *15*

    Zhūgě Liàng *15*

    Jiāng Zǐyá *17*

    Zhāng Liáng (Western Han) *17*

    Liu Bowen *19*

    What is 奇门遁甲 (Qí Mén Dùn Jiǎ)? *20*

    Five Elements *21*

    天盘 (Heaven Plate - Tiān Pán) *39*

    地盘 (Earth Plate - Dì Pán) *41*

    人盘 (Human Plate - Rén Pán) *42*

    The full picture of Qi Men chart *44*

        伏吟 (Fú Yín) Chart *44*

    空 (Emptiness - Kōng) *46*

    旬首 (Leader - Xún Shǒu) *47*

    Qi Men Dun Jia Season *51*

    Steps to plot Qi Men Dun Jia chart *52*

    拆布 (Chāi Bù) Method of Plotting Qi Men Dun Jia Chart *52*

    Divination *68*

- *Application* *69*
  - Marriage 69
  - House Renovation 69
  - Yin Fengshui 69
  - Move-in to new house 70
  - Opening Ceremony for Business 70
  - Interview or Exam 70
  - Assemble of Bed 71
  - Other forms of application 71
- *Destiny Analysis* *71*
- *Change Name* *72*
- *Fengshui* *73*
- *Religious Matter* *73*
- *What is Qi Men Life Changing Method?* *76*
- *What is divination?* *79*
- *What are the unknown circumstances?* *81*
- *Destiny Reading* *83*
- *Believing or leaving to Destiny* *84*
- *Destiny – Luck cycle* *85*
- *Bazi is diagnosis while Fengshui is prescription* *86*

How to maximize your luck **88**

- Why Destiny Reading is accurate when reading the past? 90
- How can you maximize your opportunity using Qi Men Dun Jia? 90
- What are my favourable elements? 96

History of Date Selection 99

- Sun Tzu Art of War 104
- Thirty-Six Stratagems (三十六计) 106
  - Chapter 1: Winning Stratagems (勝戰計 Shèng Zhàn Jì) 107
  - Chapter 2: Enemy Dealing Stratagems (敵戰計) 109
  - Chapter 3: Attacking Stratagems (攻戰計) 110
  - Chapter 4: Chaos Stratagems (混戰計) 111
  - Chapter 5: Proximate Stratagems (並戰計) 112
  - Chapter 6: Desperate Stratagems (敗戰計) 113

Divination Cases 116

- Case 1: House Audit 116
  - Analysis 117
- Case 2: House Audit – Child always fall sick 118
  - Analysis 119
- Case 3: Bus breakdown 120
  - Background 120
  - Analysis 121
- Case 4: Male or Female doctor 122

- Background 122
- Analysis 123

Case 5: Tour bus stuck at Yang Ming Shan, Taipei 124
- Background 124
- Analysis 125

Case 6: Sickness Diagnostic 126
- Background 126
- Analysis 127

Case 7: Colleague giving birth timing 128
- Background 128
- Analysis 129

Case 8: Colleague worrying about her health 130
- Background 130
- Analysis 131

Case 9: Haunted house 132
- Background 132
- Analysis 133

Case 10: Girlfriend left him 134
- Background 134
- Analysis 135

Case 11: Project having problem, take action 136

    Background 136

    Analysis 137

  Case 12: Parents' volunteer interview *138*

    Background 138

    Analysis 139

  Case 13: Relationship *140*

    Background 140

    Analysis 141

Bazi Cases **142**

  Breast Cancer Indicator *142*

    Case 14: Sheryl Crow (diagnosed on 2006 at age 44) 143

    Analysis 144

    Case 15: Kylie Minogue (diagnosed 2005 at 36) 145

    Analysis 146

  Case 16: Christina Applegate (diagnosed 2008 at 36) *147*

    Analysis 148

  Case 17: Judy Holliday *149*

    Analysis 150

  Case 18: Angelina Jolie *151*

    Analysis 152

  Breast Cancer Indicator – note *153*

Ability to connect with the supernatural 154

    Case 19: Date of Birth: 7th Dec 2007 at Xu hour 154

    Case 20: Date of Birth: 22nd Mar 2013 at 06:53 155

    Case 21: Nella Jones's Date of Birth 4th May 1932 at 10:30 156

Case 22: Lady Diana - At the wrong place, at the wrong time 157

Case 23: Whitney Houston - House Fengshui doesn't match her bazi. 160

Case 24: Michael Jordon - House Fengshui that helps his career. 163

Case 25: Difficulties in conceiving 167

    Analysis 168

World Cup Prediction Cases **169**

Case 26: Brazil vs Croatia 169

    Analysis 170

Case 27: Mexico vs Cameron 171

    Analysis 172

Case 28: Spain vs Holland 173

    Analysis 174

Case 29: Chile vs Australia 175

    Analysis 176

Case 30: Columbia vs Greece 177

    Analysis 178

Date Selection Cases **179**

Case 31: Marina Bay Sands Opening 179
  Background 179
  Analysis 180
Case 32: Marriage date chosen ended in divorce 184
  Background 184
  Analysis 185
Case 33: Singapore Flyer opening, ended with receivership 186
  Background 186
  Analysis 188

Comments from Clients and Students 189

Courses Available 197
  Qi Men Dun Jia for day-to-day application 197
  Advanced QMDJ 198
  Bazi QMDJ 198
  QMDJ Date Selection 199
  Road to QMDJ Practitioner Program 200

Products 201
  Qi Men Talismans 201
  5 Elephant on the Bridge 201
  Maintain Wealth Horse 202
  Peaceful 3-Ram 202

Golden Bull *202*

Qi Men home enhancement bronze elephant *203*

Chinese Character **204**

Tradition vs Simplify Chinese *204*

Pinyin Representation: *204*

Tones: *205*

Characters used in Qi Men Dun Jia *206*

Author's Note

For those who know what Qi Men Dun Jia is, they always think that Qi Men Dun Jia can only be used in battle field. In fact, some famous master even commented that Qi Men Dun Jia is not applicable in modern society. Qi Men Dun Jia had existed for more than 5,000 years and in ancient time, it can only be used by Emperor and his advisors. Those who practice without his permission will be executed.

This book is a complete revision of my first book, *Control Your Destiny by Mastering Qi Men Dun Jia*. The purpose of the revision is to give readers a more accurate perspective of Qi Men Dun Jia usage.

Among Qi Men Dun Jia practitioners, it is well known that Qi Men Dun Jia is used for divination. This book is to present other usage of Qi Men Dun Jia and how it can be used in modern society.

I have presented various case studies in this book for illustration. Please note that cases presented are actual real cases. However, readers are advised not to follow the method presented here without any proper training. Qi Men Dun Jia is powerful; it can help you but if used wrongly, it can bring undesired outcome. This is because throughout history of China, Qi Men Dun Jia has been used to bring down dynasties.

I've conducted various courses in both distant learning and classroom forms. Please feel free to contact me for signing up the courses.

Calvin Yap

Calvin_yap@yahoo.com
http://www.fengshui-hacks.com

Other books from Author:

1. Control Your Destiny by Mastering Qi Men Dun Jia (ISBN: 978-981-08-7136-9)
2. Qi Men Dun Jia (奇门遁甲) Chāi Bù (拆布) English Calendar 2011 – 2020 (ISBN: 978-981-08-7386-8)
3. Practical Application of Qi Men Dun Jia (ISBN: 978-981-08-9837-3)
4. Qi Men Dun Jia Compendium Series Volume 1 - English Chai Bu & Zhi Run Calendar 1930 – 2020 (ISBN: 978-981-07-0509-1)
5. Qi Men Dun Jia Compendium Series Volume 2 - 540 Yang Dun Chart (ISBN: 978-981-07-0510-7)
6. Qi Men Dun Jia Compendium Series Volume 3 - 540 Yin Dun Chart (ISBN: 978-981-07-0511-4)
7. FengShui at Your Fingertips (ISBN: 978-981-07-1670-7)
8. Destiny Analysis of Famous People using Qi Men Dun Jia (not available to public)

Translation by Author:

1. Basic Qi Men Dun Jia - How to become a Fengshui Master by Master Ye (ISBN: 978-981-07-1745-2)
2. Destiny Analysis Using Qi Men Dun Jia by Master Ye
3. Date Selection Using Qi Men Dun Jia by Master Ye

What is Qi Men Dun Jia

Introduction to Qi Men Dun Jia

奇门遁甲 (Qí Mén Dùn Jiǎ) is an ancient form of Chinese Meta-Physics which is still used today. Because of its name, Qi Men, which loosely translates to Mystical Door, gives a sense of mystical or magic to the people who don't know the background. Qi Men Dun Jia may be applied to business, crime-solving, marriages and matchmaking, medical divination, Feng Shui, military affairs, finding missing people, travel, personal fortune divination etc.

It was recorded in Chinese history that Qi Men Dun Jia, together with Da Liu Ren and Tai Yi Shen Shu are the epitomi peak of the Three Arts or Three Styles (三式 sān shì) in Chinese Meta-physics. It was said that these Arts can only be practice by the Emperor or their advisors. Commoners caught practicing these Three Arts run the risk of being executed!

According to legend, Qi Men Dun Jia was taught to Yellow Emperor (黃帝 Huáng Dì- 2697 BC to 2597 BC) by a fairy, 九天玄女 (Jiǔ Tiān Xuán Nǚ). During that time, Yellow Emperor was fighting against a rebel called 蚩尤 (Chī Yóu). Chī Yóu was very familiar with the art of Yin & Yang and has the capability to summon the wind and rain. It was said that his head is as strong as copper and arm is like iron (铜头铁臂) and was able to win any wars. During battle, Yellow Emperor did not have the capability to defeat him. In desperation, 九天玄女 (Jiǔ Tiān Xuán Nǚ) passed the art of Qi Men Dun Jia to Yellow Emperor. With the art of Qi Men Dun Jia, Yellow Emperor invented the 指南车 (South Pointing Chariot). Yellow Emperor used the art of Qi Men Dun Jia and South Pointing Chariot to win the war against Chī Yóu.

Zhūgě Liàng [1]

诸葛亮 (Zhūgě Liàng), 181–234 was Chancellor of Shu Han during the Three Kingdoms period of China. He is often recognized as the greatest and most accomplished strategist of his era. He was said to use the technique in Qi Men Dun Jia to win battles.

---

[1] Adopted from wikipedia

Using straw boats to borrow arrows

Before the Battle of Red Cliffs, Zhūgě Liàng visited the Wu camp to assist 周瑜 (Zhōu Yú). 周瑜 (Zhōu Yú) saw Zhūgě Liàng as a threat to Eastern Wu and was also jealous of Zhūgě Liàng 's talent. He assigned Zhūgě Liàng the task of making 100,000 arrows in ten days or face execution for failure in duties under military law. Zhūgě Liàng promised that he will finish this seemingly impossible task in three days. He requested 20 large boats; each manned by a few soldiers and filled with straw made human-like figures. Before dawn, with river fog cloaking his movements, Zhūgě Liàng deployed his ships. He ordered his soldiers to beat war drums and shout orders so as to imitate the noise of an attack.

Upon hearing the drums, the Wei soldiers rushed out to meet the "attack". Zhūgě Liàng drank wine with Lu Su in one of the boats. The Wei soldiers were unable to see through the fog and fired volleys of arrows at the sound of the drums. The straw figures were soon penetrated by many arrows, which were stuck in the straw. Zhūgě Liàng returned to Wu in triumph. After removing the arrows from the straw figures' bodies, Zhūgě Liàng discovered there were over 100,000 arrows.

It was said that Zhūgě Liàng used Qi Men Dun Jia to get the correct timing and direction of the river fog.

赤壁之戰 (Battle of Red Cliffs)

Zhūgě Liàng wanted to burn up 曹操 (Cáo Cāo)'s fleet of chained ships and knew that it could only be done by launching arrows with fire with the help of east wind. Zhūgě Liàng set up the Seven Stars Altar and prayed for the east wind. In a short time, the east wind was in full force. Zhūgě Liàng used Qi Men to predict the timing of the east wind and uses the Seven Stars Altar to buy time and to create mystery of the entire strategy.

Jiāng Zǐyá [2]

姜子牙 (Jiāng Zǐyá), was a Chinese historical and legendary figure who resided next to the Weishui River about 3,000 years ago. The region was the feudal estate of King Wen of Zhou. The last ruler of the Shang dynasty, King Zhou of Shang (16th - 11th century BC) was a tyrannical and debauched slave owner who spent his days carousing with his favourite concubine Daji and mercilessly executing or punishing upright officials and all others who objected to his ways. Jiāng Zǐyá had once served the Shang king and had come to hate him with all his heart. He was an expert in military affairs (i.e. Qi Men Dun Jia) and hoped that some day someone would call on him to help overthrown the king. He waited and waited till he was 80 years old, continuing placidly with his fishing in a tributary of the Weihe River (near today's Xi'an) using a barbless hook or even no hook at all, on the theory that the fish would come to him of their own volition when they were ready.

King Wen of the Zhou state, (central Shaanxi), found Jiāng fishing. King Wen, following the advice of his father and grandfather before him, was in search of talented people. In fact, he had been told by his grandfather, the Grand Duke of Zhou, that one day a sage would appear to help rule the Zhou state.

When King Wen saw Jiang, at first sight, he felt that this was an unusual old man and began to converse with him. He discovered that this white-haired fisherman was actually an astute political thinker and military strategist. This, he felt, must be the man his grandfather was waiting for. He took Jiang in his coach to the court and appointed him prime minister and gave him the title Jiang Taigongwang ("The Great Duke's Hope", or "The expected of the Great Duke") in reference to a prophetic dream Danfu, grandfather of Wenwang, had had many years before. This was later shortened to Jiang Taigong.

Zhāng Liáng (Western Han)[3]

張良(Zhāng Liáng) 262 BC – 189 BC, was a strategist and statesman of the early Han Dynasty period of Chinese history. He is also known as one

---

[2] Adopted from wikipedia

[3] Adopted from wikipedia

of the "Three Heroes of the early Han Dynasty" (漢初三傑), along with Han Xin and Xiao He. Zhāng Liáng contributed greatly to the founding of the Han Dynasty.

To avenge the fall of his native state, Zhāng Liáng dedicated his efforts to hire assassins to kill Qin Shi Huang. Qin Shi Huang survived the assassination attempt, after which he issued an order for the arrest of Zhang Liang. As a wanted man by the government, Zhāng Liáng travelled to Xiapi and stayed there for some time, using fake identities to evade the authorities. One day, Zhāng Liáng took a stroll at the Yishui Bridge and met an old man there. The man walked towards Zhāng and chucked his shoe down the bridge on purpose, after which he yelled at Zhāng, "Hey boy, go down and fetch me my shoe!" Zhāng Liáng was astonished and unhappy but he obeyed silently. The old man then lifted his foot and ordered Zhāng Liáng to put on the shoe for him. Zhāng Liáng was furious but he controlled his temper and meekly obliged. The old man did not show any sign of gratitude and walked away in laughter. The old man came back after walking a distance and praised Zhāng Liáng, "This child can be taught!" and he asked Zhāng Liáng to meet him at the bridge again at dawn five days later. Zhāng Liáng was confused but he agreed.

Five days later, Zhāng Liáng rushed to the bridge at the stroke of dawn but the old man was already waiting for him there. The old man chided him, "How can you be late for a meeting with an elderly man? Come back again five days later!" Zhāng Liáng tried his best to be punctual the second time but the old man still arrived earlier than him, and he was scorned by the old man once more and told to return again five days later. The third time, Zhāng Liáng went to the bridge at midnight and waited until the old man appeared. This time, the old man was impressed with Zhāng Liáng's fortitude that he presented Zhāng Liáng with a book, saying, "You can become the tutor of a ruler after reading this book. In ten years time the world will become chaotic, and you can use your knowledge from this book to bring peace and prosperity to the empire. Meet me again thirteen years later. I'm the yellow rock at the foot of Mount Gucheng." The old man was Huang Shigong (黃石公; aka "Yellow Rock Old Man") of the legendary "Four Haos of Mount Shang" (商山四皓), a group of four reclusive wise men. The book was titled The Art of War by Taigong (太公兵法) and believed to be the Six Secret Teachings by Jiāng Zǐyá.

Liu Bowen

Liu Ji (1311 - 1375), style name Bowen, was a key military consultant of Zhu Yuanzhang, the founder of Ming dynasty. It was said that Liu Bowen used Qi Men Dun Jia skill to bring the Ming dynasty to the throne.

Mao Zedong

毛泽东 Máo Zédōng (December 26, 1893 – September 9, 1976) was a Chinese revolutionary, political theorist and communist leader. He led the People's Republic of China (PRC) from its establishment in 1949 until his death in 1976. It was rumor that Mao actually used Qi Men Dun Jia to win battle with Kuomintang. In some of the battles, Mao actually dictated the actual timing and direction for the troop to be deployed, which is the signature of Qi Men Dun Jia.

Basic Concept

What is 奇门遁甲 (Qí Mén Dùn Jiǎ)?

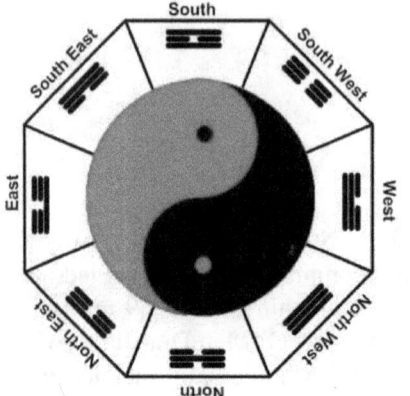

奇门遁甲 (Qí Mén Dùn Jiǎ) offers a map of Chinese Hour. 奇门遁甲 (Qí Mén Dùn Jiǎ) uses Post-Heaven Trigram or Ba Gua as its basis.

A 奇门遁甲 (Qí Mén Dùn Jiǎ) chart will provide information with regards to Heaven, Earth and Man interaction. (天时，地利，人和). The Heaven, Earth and Man interaction is the most important concept in Chinese Meta-Physics. If the chart shows support from Heaven, Earth and Man means it is an auspicious chart. In Sun Zi art of war, it was stated: "天时、地利、人和，三者不得，虽胜有殃", which means, if there is no support from Heaven, Earth and Man, even you win the war, there will be calamity.

Confucius definitions of 天时、地利、人和 are:
1. 天时 (Heaven): if now is spring then don't bother about summer or winter's matter.

2. 地利 (Earth): if there is a small lake, then just say go to a small lake to swim. Don't say you are swimming at big river.

3. 人和 (Man): if there is 5-6 adults then don't say that there is more than 100 people.

In a nutshell, it means that a person should make full use of the Heaven, Earth and Man elements in the natural state (i.e. follow the flow of nature)

There are various methods of plotting 奇门遁甲 (Qí Mén Dùn Jiǎ) chart. The most popular ones are Chāi Bù (拆布) and Zhí Rùn (直闰) methods. There are other methods not mentioned here but that doesn't imply that they are not used. In addition, there might be slight practice variances even within Chāi Bù or Zhí Rùn method between Masters.

Five Elements

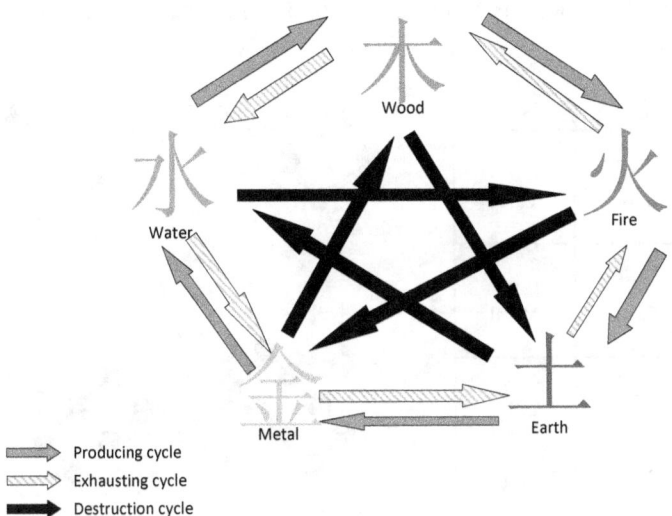

The concept of the Five Elements (五行) is the most basic fundamental as well as the most important concept to remember and to understand the basic art of metaphysics. Ancient Chinese Sage derived that the universe consists of five building blocks. They are Earth, Metal, Water, Wood and Fire. Each element has its own attributes and characteristics. These five elements follow the law of nature as describe below:

Wood produces Fire, exhausts Water and controls Earth.
Fire produces Earth, exhausts Wood and controls Metal.
Earth produces Metal, exhausts Fire and controls Water.
Metal produces Water, exhausts Earth and controls Wood.
Water produces Wood, exhausts Metal and controls Fire.

Luo Shu (Magic Squares)

According to the legend, it was said that a giant tortoise emerged from the river. Inscribed on its back were circular dots in 3x3 grid pattern. It is also known as Magic Squares.

	SE	South	SW	
East	4 Wood	9 Fire	2 Earth	
	3 Wood	5 Earth	7 Metal	West
	8 Earth	1 Water	6 Metal	
	NE	North	NW	

Ba Gua (Trigram)

It was claimed that Fu Xi is the person who invented the Ba Gua. There are 2 types of Ba Gua; Pre-Heaven and Post-Heaven. The tips to memorize the Ba Gua are as follow:

Ba Gua	Symbol	Memorizing (in Chinese)	Translation
乾 qián (Father)		乾 qián 三 sān 连 lián	Qián is 3 links
兑 duì (Youngest Daughter)		兑 duì 上 shàng 缺 quē	Duì lack of top
離 lí (Middle Daughter)		離 lí 中 zhōng 虚 xū	Lí middle void
震 zhèn (Eldest Son)		震 zhèn 仰 yǎng 孟 yú	Zhèn is upward-facing jar
巽 xùn (Eldest Daughter)		巽 xùn 下 xià 断 duàn	Xùn is broken off at the bottom
坎 kǎn (Middle Son)		坎 kǎn 中 zhōng 满 mǎn	Kǎn is full in the middle
艮 gèn (Youngest Son)		艮 gèn 覆 fù 碗 wǎn	Gèn is upside down bowl
坤 kūn (Mother)		坤 kūn 六 liù 断 duàn	Kūn is 6 broken-off line

In Chinese Meta-Physics, the Post-Heaven Ba Gua is mostly used. The Pre-Heaven Ba Gua is used to supplement any formula if needed.

The lines were derived from the Taiji where the Chinese believed that the universe is made of positive and negative energy balancing each other. When there is sunlight, there will be darkness; when there is strong, there is weak.

The Taiji shows that everything is in virtuous cycle with the blending of Yin and Yang influences. This is the inter-locking black and white as shown in the Taiji symbol. The stronger element is denoted as Yang. Therefore, sunlight is Yang while darkness is Yin. Movement is Yang and stationary is Yin. Therefore, in Feng Shui, mountain is considered as Yin, while water is considered as Yang. In a natural environment, water collects in mountain and forms river. Therefore, it can be said that mountain produce water.

In Taiji you will notice that in Yin there is Yang and in Yang there is Yin. Looking at the Taiji chart, you will find that within black there is white and within white there is black. This is the meaning. The Taiji is further derived into solid and broken line. The solid line denotes Yang or Male and the broken line denotes Yin or Female.

▬▬▬ This is a Yang line and it denotes Male. ▬▬ ▬▬ This is a Yin line and it denotes Female. The solid line and broken line are further arranged to form the Ba Gua.

The Pre-Heaven Ba Gua layout on 3 X 3 grids is as follow:

兌 duì Youngest Daughter Metal, 4 Lake	乾 qián Father Metal, 9 Heaven	巽 xùn Eldest Daughter Wood, 2 Wind
離 lí Middle Daughter Fire, 3 Fire	5	坎 kǎn Middle Son Water, 7 Water
震 zhèn Eldest Son Wood, 8 Thunder	坤 kūn Mother Earth, 1 Earth	艮 gèn Youngest Son Earth, 6 Mountain

The Post-Heaven Ba Gua layout on 3 X 3 grids is as follow:

巽 xùn Eldest Daughter Wood, 4 Wind	離 lí Middle Daughter Fire, 9 Fire	坤 kūn Mother Earth, 2 Earth
震 zhèn Eldest Son Wood, 3 Thunder	5	兑 duì Youngest Daughter Metal, 7 Lake
艮 gèn Youngest Son Earth, 8 Mountain	坎 kǎn Middle Son Water, 1 Water	乾 qián Father Metal, 6 Heaven

Qi Men Dun Jia uses both Pre & Post-Heaven Ba Gua as references. Charts are plotted using the Post-Heaven Ba Gua as a base.

九宫八卦图 (9 Palaces 8 Trigram chart - Jiǔ Gōng Bā Guà Tú)

The 9 Palaces 8 Trigram is basically the Post-Heaven Trigram arrangement. Each Trigram is called Palace (宫) and has associated element and direction. It is used to determine the state of interaction between other elements of Qi Men. In addition, it is also being used to determine the direction or timing of certain things happening or about to happen.

The following chart shows the element of each palace and the associated family members and numbers:

	SE (东南)	South (正南)	SW (西南)	
	4, 5 巽四宫 3, 8 (Xun 4) Eldest Daughter Wood	3, 9 离九宫 2, 7 (Li 9) Middle Daughter Fire	坤二宫 2, 8 (Kun 2) 5, 10 Mother/Lady Master Earth	
East (正东)	3, 4 震三宫 3, 8 (Zhen 3) Eldest Son Wood	中宫 (Middle 5) Earth	兑七宫 2, 7 (Dui 7) 4, 9 Youngest Daughter Metal	West (正西)
	7, 8 艮八宫 5, 10 (Gen 8) Youngest Son Earth	1, 6 坎一宫 (Kan 1) Middle Son Water	乾六宫 1, 6 (Qian 6) 4, 9 Father/Male Master Metal	
	NE (东北)	North (正北)	NW (西北)	

Associated family members can be used in prediction to see what's happening (e.g. sickness or what event is happening to this person). The numbers can be used to predict for lottery or certain things that require figures (e.g. amount of compensation).

Relationship between palaces

The following shows the five elements' relationship between palaces and how to derive auspicious and inauspicious. This is used when evaluating relationship between 2 palaces. For example, comparison is done on items like Heavenly Stems, 八神 (8 God - Bā Shén), 九星 (Jiǔ Xīng) or 八门 (Bā Mén) in Kan 1 Palace (which is Water) against items in Kun 2 Palace (which is Earth).

Kan 1 Palace (North, Water element)

Other Palace	Element	Relationship	Auspiciousness
Kun 2 (SW)	Earth	Earth controls Water. Kun 2 controls Kan 1.	Inauspicious
Zhen 3 (East)	Wood	Water gives birth to Wood. Kan 1 supports Zhen 3.	Auspicious
Xun 4 (SE)	Wood	Water gives birth to Wood. Kan 1 supports Xun 4.	Auspicious
Qian 6 (NW)	Metal	Metal gives birth to Water. Qian 6 supports Kan 1.	Auspicious
Dui 7 (West)	Metal	Metal gives birth to Water. Dui 7 supports Kan 1.	Auspicious
Gen 8 (NE)	Earth	Earth controls Water. Gen 8 controls Kan 1.	Inauspicious
Li 9 (South)	Fire	Water controls Fire. Kan 1 controls Li 9.	Inauspicious

Kun 2 Palace (South West, Earth element)

Other Palace	Element	Relationship	Auspiciousness
Kan 1 (North)	Water	Earth controls Water. Kun 2 controls Kan 1.	Inauspicious
Zhen 3 (East)	Wood	Wood controls Earth. Zhen 3 controls Kun 2.	Inauspicious
Xun 4 (SE)	Wood	Wood controls Earth. Xun 4 controls Kun 2.	Inauspicious
Qian 6 (NW)	Metal	Earth gives birth to Metal. Kun 2 supports Qian 6.	Auspicious
Dui 7 (West)	Metal	Earth gives birth to Metal. Kun 2 supports Dui 7.	Auspicious
Gen 8 (NE)	Earth	Same element. Gen 8 supports Kun 2.	Auspicious
Li 9 (South)	Fire	Fire gives birth to Earth. Li 9 supports Kun 2.	Auspicious

Zhen 3 Palace (East, Wood element)

Other Palace	Element	Relationship	Auspiciousness
Kan 1 (North)	Water	Water gives birth to Wood. Kan 1 supports Zhen 3.	Auspicious
Kun 2 (SW)	Earth	Wood controls Earth. Zhen 3 controls Kun 2.	Inauspicious
Xun 4 (SE)	Wood	Same element. Xun 4 supports Zhen 3.	Auspicious
Qian 6 (NW)	Metal	Metal controls Wood. Qian 6 controls Zhen 3.	Inauspicious
Dui 7 (West)	Metal	Metal controls Wood. Dui 7 controls Zhen 3.	Inauspicious
Gen 8 (NE)	Earth	Wood controls Earth. Zhen 3 controls Gen 8.	Inauspicious
Li 9 (South)	Fire	Wood gives birth to Fire. Zhen 3 supports Li 9.	Auspicious

Xun 4 Palace (South East, Wood element)

Other Palace	Element	Relationship	Auspiciousness
Kan 1 (North)	Water	Water gives birth to Wood. Kan 1 supports Xun 4.	Auspicious
Kun 2 (SW)	Earth	Wood controls Earth. Xun 4 controls Kun 2.	Inauspicious
Zhen 3 (East)	Wood	Same element. Zhen 3 supports Xun 4.	Auspicious
Qian 6 (NW)	Metal	Metal controls Wood. Qian 6 controls Xun 4.	Inauspicious
Dui 7 (West)	Metal	Metal controls Wood. Dui 7 controls Xun 4.	Inauspicious
Gen 8 (NE)	Earth	Wood controls Earth. Xun 4 controls Gen 8.	Inauspicious
Li 9 (South)	Fire	Wood gives birth to Fire. Xun 4 supports Li 9.	Auspicious

Qian 6 Palace (North West, Metal element)

Other Palace	Element	Relationship	Auspiciousness
Kan 1 (North)	Water	Metal gives birth to Water. Qian 6 supports Kan 1.	Auspicious
Kun 2 (SW)	Earth	Earth gives birth to Metal. Kun 2 support Qian 6.	Auspicious
Zhen 3 (East)	Wood	Metal controls Wood. Qian 6 controls Zhen 3.	Inauspicious
Xun 4 (SE)	Wood	Metal controls Wood. Qian 6 controls Xun 4.	Inauspicious
Dui 7 (West)	Metal	Same element. Dui 7 supports Qian 6.	Auspicious
Gen 8 (NE)	Earth	Earth gives birth to Metal. Gen 8 supports Qian 6.	Auspicious
Li 9 (South)	Fire	Fire controls Metal. Li 9 controls Qian 6.	Inauspicious

Dui 7 Palace (West, Metal element)

Other Palace	Element	Relationship	Auspiciousness
Kan 1 (North)	Water	Metal gives birth to Water. Dui 7 supports Kan 1.	Auspicious
Kun 2 (SW)	Earth	Earth gives birth to Metal. Kun 2 supports Dui 7.	Auspicious
Zhen 3 (East)	Wood	Metal controls Wood. Dui 7 controls Zhen 3.	Inauspicious
Xun 4 (SE)	Wood	Metal controls Wood. Dui 7 controls Xun 4.	Inauspicious
Qian 6 (NW)	Metal	Same element. Dui 7 supports Qian 6.	Auspicious
Gen 8 (NE)	Earth	Earth gives birth to Metal. Gen 8 supports Dui 7.	Auspicious
Li 9 (South)	Fire	Fire controls Metal. Li 9 controls Dui 7.	Inauspicious

Gen 8 Palace (North East, Earth element)

Other Palace	Element	Relationship	Auspiciousness
Kan 1 (North)	Water	Earth controls Water. Gen 8 controls Kan 1.	Inauspicious
Kun 2 (SW)	Earth	Same element. Kun 2 supports Gen 8.	Auspicious
Zhen 3 (East)	Wood	Wood controls Earth. Zhen 3 controls Gen 8.	Inauspicious
Xun 4 (SE)	Wood	Wood controls Earth. Xun 4 controls Gen 8.	Inauspicious
Qian 6 (NW)	Metal	Earth gives birth to Metal. Gen 8 supports Qian 6.	Auspicious
Dui 7 (West)	Metal	Earth gives birth to Metal. Gen 8 supports Dui 7.	Auspicious
Li 9 (South)	Fire	Fire gives birth to Earth. Li 9 Supports Gen 8.	Auspicious

Li 9 Palace (South, Fire element)

Other Palace	Element	Relationship	Auspiciousness
Kan 1 (North)	Water	Water controls Fire. Kan 1 controls Li 9.	Inauspicious
Kun 2 (SW)	Earth	Fire gives birth to Earth. Li 9 supports Kun 2.	Auspicious
Zhen 3 (East)	Wood	Wood gives birth to Fire. Zhen 3 supports Li 9.	Auspicious
Xun 4 (SE)	Wood	Wood gives birth to Fire. Xun 4 supports Li 9.	Auspicious
Qian 6 (NW)	Metal	Fire controls Metal. Li 9 controls Qian 6.	Inauspicious
Dui 7 (West)	Metal	Fire controls Metal. Li 9 controls Dui 7.	Inauspicious
Gen 8 (NE)	Earth	Fire gives birth to Earth. Gen 8 supports Li 9.	Auspicious

Sickness

The 用神 (Useful God - Yòng Shén) for sickness is 天芮 (Tiān Ruì) Star. The palace where 天芮 (Tiān Ruì) Star is indicates what type of sickness a person has.

The type of sickness depends on the palace where 天芮 (Tiān Ruì) Star is:

Palace	Sickness
Kan 1	• Kidney • Urinal track • Lower abdomen
Kun 2	• Stomach • Intestine • Spleen • Internal organ • Right arm
Zhen 3	• Liver • Gall bladder • Left rib • Muscle • Left breast • Waist
Xun 4	• Shoulder • Neck • Left arm
Qian 6	• Heart • Internal organs • Right foot
Dui 7	• Lung • Right rib • Throat • Mouth • Right breast • Skin
Gen 8	• Left foot
Li 9	• Heart • Arteries • Head

十天干 (10 Heavenly Stems - Shí Tiān Gān)

The 10 Heavenly Stems are 甲 (Jia), 乙 (Yi), 丙 (Bing), 丁 (Ding), 戊 (Wu), 己 (Ji), 庚 (Geng), 辛 (Xin), 壬 (Ren), 癸 (Gui). In Qi Men Dun Jia, 甲 (Jia) is the head of 10 Heavenly Stems. 甲 (Jia) is Wood element and is most afraid to meet Geng Metal. 甲 (Jia), the general must be protected. Therefore, in Qi Men Dun Jia chart, 甲 (Jia) is hidden from being hurt. That's the Dun Jia (遁甲) part, means to hide the Jia.

In Qi Men Dun Jia, there is the Sān Qí Liù Yí (三奇六仪) concept. The San Qi (three mystical or three noblemen) are 乙 (Yi), 丙 (Bing), 丁 (Ding). Yi is Jia's sister, because Yi and Geng can combine, Jia can "marry" Yi to Geng so that Geng won't attack Jia. Bing and Ding are Fire element. In 5-elements, Wood gives birth to Fire. Therefore, Bing and Ding are children of Jia. Children have the duty to protect their parents. In 5-elements, Fire restricts Metal. Hence, Bing and Ding are part of San Qi because the three have close relationship with Jia. Therefore, the three of them are called San Qi or three noblemen. In Qi Men Dun Jia, the auspicious are the San Qi (Ding, Bing and Yi) and inauspicious are the Liu Yi (Wu, Ji, Geng, Xin, Ren, Gui).

乙 (Yi): represents woman, doctor of Traditional Chinese Medicine, winding, zigzag.

丙 (Bing): represents fire, red colour, 3rd party (male)

丁 (Ding): represents faint fire, light red colour, 3rd party (female)

戊 (Wu): represents wealth, capital (money), block or stuck

己 (Ji): represents earth or soil, hills.

庚 (Geng): represents metal, hardware, police.

辛 (Xin): represents small items, mole, prize or trophy, mistake (action)

壬 (Ren): represents clear or clean water, movement.

癸 (Gui): represents dirty water, puddle (of water).

The matching of 10 Heavenly Stems in Qi Men Dun Jia are:

乙 (Yi)	庚 (Geng)
丙 (Bing)	辛 (Xin)
丁 (Ding)	壬 (Ren)
戊 (Wu)	癸 (Gui)
己 (Ji)	戊 (Wu)

60 JiaZi and calendar

The calendar system that we all know is called Gregorian calendar, Western calendar, or Christian calendar. It is based on the orbit of the earth around the sun. One year is equivalent to 365.25 days.

The Chinese has 2 calendars; one is called Lunisolar and another is called the Xia Calendar, Solar Calendar, Farmer Calendar, JiaZi Calendar or Thousand Years Calendar. The Lunisolar Calendar is based on the cycle of the moon around the earth with adjustment to Solar Calendar. The first day of first month of a particular year in Lunisolar Calendar is also known as Chinese New Year.

In Chinese Meta-physics, the Xia Calendar is used. It is called Xia Calendar because it was invented during the Xia dynasty. It is called Solar Calendar because it is solely based on the orbit of the earth around the sun. It is also called the Farmer Calendar because it indicates the 24 Sub-Season (二十四节气) throughout the year so that the farmer knows when to start planting and harvesting.

The key element of Xia Calendar is that it uses the pairing of Heavenly Stem and Earthly Branches to represent the Year, Month, Day and Hour. There are 10 Heavenly Stems – 5 Yang Stems and 5 Yin Stems. There are 12 Earthly Branches – 6 Yang Branches and 6 Yin Branches. Yang Stem can only pair with Yang Branch and Yin Stem can only pair with Yin Branch; starting from Jia Zi and ends with Gui Hai which makes 60 pairs. Therefore, the pairing is also called **60 JiaZi** (六十甲子). The list of 60 JiaZi pairing is as follow:

甲(Jia) 子(Zi)	甲(Jia) 戌(Xu)	甲(Jia) 申(Shen)	甲(Jia) 午(Wu)	甲(Jia) 辰(Chen)	甲(Jia) 寅(Yin)
乙(Yi) 丑(Chou)	乙(Yi) 亥(Hai)	乙(Yi) 酉(You)	乙(Yi) 未(Wei)	乙(Yi) 巳(Si)	乙(Yi) 卯(Mao)
丙(Bing) 寅(Yin)	丙(Bing) 子(Zi)	丙(Bing) 戌(Xu)	丙(Bing) 申(Shen)	丙(Bing) 午(Wu)	丙(Bing) 辰(Chen)
丁(Ding) 卯(Mao)	丁(Ding) 丑(Chou)	丁(Ding) 亥(Hai)	丁(Ding) 酉(You)	丁(Ding) 未(Wei)	丁(Ding) 巳(Si)
戊(Wu) 辰(Chen)	戊(Wu) 寅(Yin)	戊(Wu) 子(Zi)	戊(Wu) 戌(Xu)	戊(Wu) 申(Shen)	戊(Wu) 午(Wu)
己(Ji) 巳(Si)	己(Ji) 卯(Mao)	己(Ji) 丑(Chou)	己(Ji) 亥(Hai)	己(Ji) 酉(You)	己(Ji) 未(Wei)
庚(Geng) 午(Wu)	庚(Geng) 辰(Chen)	庚(Geng) 寅(Yin)	庚(Geng) 子(Zi)	庚(Geng) 戌(Xu)	庚(Geng) 申(Shen)
辛(Xin) 未(Wei)	辛(Xin) 巳(Si)	辛(Xin) 卯(Mao)	辛(Xin) 丑(Chou)	辛(Xin) 亥(Hai)	辛(Xin) 酉(You)
壬(Ren) 申(Shen)	壬(Ren) 午(Wu)	壬(Ren) 辰(Chen)	壬(Ren) 寅(Yin)	壬(Ren) 子(Zi)	壬(Ren) 戌(Xu)
癸(Gui) 酉(You)	癸(Gui) 未(Wei)	癸(Gui) 巳(Si)	癸(Gui) 卯(Mao)	癸(Gui) 丑(Chou)	癸(Gui) 亥(Hai)

The Year, Month, Day and Hour runs from Jia Zi to Gui Hai and then starts from Jia Zi again. That's why it is also called Jia Zi Calendar or Thousand Years Calendar because it never ends.

The hour representation is as follow:

Earthly Branches	Time
子 (Zi)	23:00 – 00:59
丑 (Chou)	01:00 – 02:59
寅 (Yin)	03:00 – 04:59
卯 (Mao)	05:00 – 06:59
辰 (Chen)	07:00 – 08:59
巳 (Si)	09:00 – 10:59
午 (Wu)	11:00 – 12:59
未 (Wei)	13:00 – 14:59
申 (Shen)	15:00 – 16:59
酉 (You)	17:00 – 18:59
戌 (Xu)	19:00 – 20:59
亥 (Hai)	21:00 – 22:59

So, 25th July 2011 at 20:00 is represented as follow:

Hour	Day	Month	Year
戊(Wu)	辛(Xin)	乙(Yi)	辛(Xin)
戌(Xu)	巳(Si)	未(Wei)	卯(Mao)

Note: Wu Xu hour is from 19:00 – 20:59.

In addition, the year changes after 立春 (Beginning of Spring - Lì Chūn). For example, in 2011, 立春 starts on 4th Feb 12:32. Therefore, those born on 3rd Feb are born in the year of Tiger (Geng Yin) and those born after 4th Feb 12:32 are born in the year of Rabbit (Xin Mao).

八神 (8 God - Bā Shén)

Ancient people said that Bā Shén represents the heaven or god. Bā Shén consists of: 值符 (Zhí Fú), 螣蛇 (Téng Shé), 太阴 (Tài Yīn), 六合 (Liù Hé), 白虎 (Bái Hǔ), 玄武 (Xuán Wǔ), 九地 (Jiǔ Dì), 九天 (Jiǔ Tiān).

Bā Shén has no original placement or 伏吟 (Fú Yín).

The auspicious Shén (Gods) are: 值符 (Zhí Fú), 太阴 (Tài Yīn), 六合 (Liù Hé), 九地 (Jiǔ Dì) and 九天 (Jiǔ Tiān).

The inauspicious Shén (Gods) are: 螣蛇 (Téng Shé), 玄武 (Xuán Wǔ), 白虎 (Bái Hǔ).

值符 (Zhí Fú): represents authority, authoritative, leader, leadership, boss, higher management, steady, valuable and precious.

螣蛇 (Téng Shé): vexed, worried, fake, false, cunning, tricky, active (like to move), agile, nimble, skeptical, nerve-racking nature, absent-minded, Schizophrenia problem.

太阴 (Tài Yīn): dark, gloomy, shadow, cloudy, gloomy, overcast, sinister, treacherous, incognito, does thing that nobody is aware of, private (character), introvert, gentle and quiet.

六合 (Liù Hé): marriage, intermediary, medium, cooperate, evidence, proof, testimony, amiable, communicator.

白虎 (Bái Hǔ): fierce, ferocious, terrible, fearful, natural disaster, traffic accident, tussle, bad-temper, temperamental, impatient, short-tempered, firm, unyielding, spirited, strong.

玄武 (Xuán Wǔ): unexpected financial loss, thief, fake, false, petty people, like to argue and don't like to admit defeat, want face.

九地 (Jiǔ Dì): slow, melancholy, depressed, slow-moving, the mother earth, low, solid, firm, honest person.

九天 (Jiǔ Tiān): tall, sky, Western Paradise (heaven), high objective, extrovert, impulsive, impatient.

天盘 (Heaven Plate - Tiān Pán)

The Tiān Pán consists of 九星 (Jiǔ Xīng) or 9 Stars. They are 天心 (Tiān Xīn), 天蓬 (Tiān Péng), 天任 (Tiān Rèn), 天冲 (Tiān Chōng), 天辅 (Tiān Fǔ), 天英 (Tiān Yīng), 天禽 (Tiān Qín), 天芮 (Tiān Ruì), 天柱 (Tiān Zhù). This is the **Heaven** (天时) aspect of Heaven, Earth & Man interaction (天时地利人和)

The original placement or 伏吟 (Fú Yín) of 九星 (Jiǔ Xīng) in the 9 Palaces is as follow:

	SE (东南)	South (正南)	SW (西南)	
	天辅 (Tiān Fǔ) 巽四宫 (Xun 4)	天英 (Tiān Yīng) 离九宫 Li 9	天芮 (Tiān Ruì) 坤二宫 (Kun 2)	
East (正东)	天冲 (Tiān Chōng) 震三宫 (Zhen 3)	天禽 (Tiān Qín) 中宫 (Middle)	天柱 (Tiān Zhù) 兑七宫 (Dui 7)	West (正西)
	天任 (Tiān Rèn) 艮八宫 (Gen 8)	天蓬 (Tiān Péng) 坎一宫 (Kan 1)	天心 (Tiān Xīn) 乾六宫 (Qian 6)	
	NE (东北)	North (正北)	NW (西北)	

Note: In Qi Men Dun Jia the middle palace is not used, 天禽 (Tiān Qín) will move to Kun 2 Palace. For charting, 天禽 (Tiān Qín) will be together with 天芮 (Tiān Ruì). The auspicious Xīng (Stars) are: 天辅 (Tiān Fǔ), 天禽 (Tiān Qín) and 天心 (Tiān Xīn).

The moderate auspicious Xīng (Stars) are: 天冲 (Tiān Chōng) and 天任 (Tiān Rèn).

The inauspicious Xīng (Stars) are: 天英 (Tiān Yīng), 天芮 (Tiān Ruì), 天柱 (Tiān Zhù) and 天蓬 (Tiān Péng).

天心 (Tiān Xīn): also known as 武曲 (Wǔ Qǔ) star, timely at NW Qian 6 Palace, Yin Star, Metal element. It represents doctor, round object, scheming person.

天蓬 (Tiān Péng): also known as 贪狼 (Tān Láng) star, timely at Kan 1 Palace, Yang Star, Water element. It represents huge wealth loosing, big robber, murderer, corruption violator, lechery, fat, at the same time it also represent wisdom and intelligence, marshal, able to handle big matters.

天任 (Tiān Rèn): also known as 左辅 (Zuǒ Fǔ) star, timely at NE Gen 8 Palace and a Yang Star. It is Earth element and represents auspiciousness, kind, honest, frank and well-behaved person.

天冲 (Tiān Chōng): also known as 禄存 (Lù Cún) star, timely at East Zhen 3 Palace and a Yang Star. It is a Wood element and represents athlete, a person who practice martial art, worrier, impulsive, do things speedily.

天辅 (Tiān Fǔ): also known as 文曲 (Wén Qǔ) star, timely at SE Xun 4 Palace and a Yang Star. It is Wood element and represents wisdom, civilization and education, teacher, examination officer, people with culture and pretty.

天英 (Tiān Yīng): also known as 右弼 (Yòu Bì) star, timely at South Li 9 Palace and a Yin Star. It is Fire element and represents strong characters, bright/promising and blood related issue.

天禽 (Tiān Qín): also known as 廉贞 (Lián Zhēn) star, timely at middle 5 Palace, therefore being checked-in to Kun 2 Palace. As such, 天禽 (Tiān Qín) is always together with 天芮 (Tiān Ruì) Star. It is a Yang Star. It is Earth element and represents honest, frank, head of hundreds Officer, loyal and has the wisdom to handle big matters.

天芮 (Tiān Ruì): also known as 巨门 (Jù Mén) star, timely at SW Kun 2 Palace and a Yin Star. It is Earth element and represents illness, issues, student, religious and Meta-physics.

天柱 (Tiān Zhù): also known as 破军 (Pò Jūn) star, timely at West Dui 7 Palace and a Yin Star. It is Metal element and represents adverse calamity, ruined, dispute, gossip, scandal, petty people and lawsuit.

地盘 (Earth Plate - Dì Pán)

The Di Pan consists of the Post-Heaven Trigram or Ba Gua and 12 Earthly Branches. The placement in the 九宫八卦图 (9 Palaces 8 Trigram chart) is as follow:

	SE (东南)	South (正南)	SW (西南)	
East (正东)	巳 (Si) 巽四宫 (Xun 4) 辰 (Chen)	午 (Wu) 离九宫 (Li 9)	未 (Wei) 坤二宫 (Kun 2) 申 (Shen)	
	卯 (Mao) 震三宫 (Zhen 3)	中宫 (Middle 5)	酉 (You) 兑七宫 (Dui 7)	West (正西)
	寅 (Yin) 艮八宫 (Gen 8) 丑 (Chou)	坎一宫 (Kan 1) 子 (Zi)	戌 (Xu) 乾六宫 (Qian 6) 亥 (Hai)	
	NE (东北)	North (正北)	NW (西北)	

This is the **Earth** (地利) aspect of Heaven, Earth & Man interaction (天时地利人和). The Earthly Branches are used to determine the timing of events. For example, Yin at Gen 8 Palace can represent Yin Year, Yin Month, Yin Day or Yin Hour.

The Earthly Branches were also used to break down the 2-hours per Earthly Branches into 10 minutes each. For example, an event happened at 12:30, 12:30 is at 午 (Wu) hour. 午 (Wu) hour is between 11:00 – 13:00. So, 11:00 is at Li 9 Palace where 午 (Wu) hour starts. 未 (Wei), which is at Kun 2 Palace, will be 11:10. 申 (Shen) at Kun 2 Palace will be 11:20 etc. 12:00 will be at Kan 1 Palace. Therefore, 12:30 is at Zhen 3 Palace. You can then read the information in Zhen 3 Palace to deduce the event.

人盘 (Human Plate - Rén Pán)

The Rén Pán consists of 八门 (Bā Mén) or 8-door. They are 开门 (Kāi Mén), 休门 (Xiū Mén), 生门 (Shēng Mén), 伤门 (Shāng Mén), 杜门 (Dù Mén), 景门 (Jǐng Mén), 死门 (Sǐ Mén), 惊门 (Jīng Mén). This is the **Man** (人和) aspect of Heaven, Earth & Man interaction (天时地利人和).

The original placement or 伏吟 (Fú Yín) of Ba Men in the 9 Palaces is as follow:

	SE (东南)	South (正南)	SW (西南)	
	巽四宫 (Xun 4) 杜门 (Dù Mén)	离九宫 (Li 9) 景门 (Jǐng Mén)	坤二宫 (Kun 2) 死门 (Sǐ Mén)	
East (正东)	震三宫 (Zhen 3) 伤门 (Shāng Mén)	中宫 (Middle)	兑七宫 (Dui 7) 惊门 (Jīng Mén)	West (正西)
	艮八宫 (Gen 8) 生门 (Shēng Mén)	坎一宫 (Kan 1) 休门 (Xiū Mén)	乾六宫 (Qian 6) 开门 (Kāi Mén)	
	NE (东北)	North (正北)	NW (西北)	

Auspicious Men are 开门 (Kāi Mén), 休门 (Xiū Mén) and 生门 (Shēng Mén). The moderate Men are 杜门 (Dù Mén) and 景门 (Jǐng Mén). The inauspicious Men are 死门 (Sǐ Mén), 伤门 (Shāng Mén) and 惊门 (Jīng Mén).

Man (人和) aspect of Heaven, Earth & Man interaction (天时地利人和).

开门 (Kāi Mén): is Metal element and timely is at NW Qian 6 Palace. It represents leader, father, higher authority, capital (country), judge, job, career, shop front, factory, and company.

休门 (Xiū Mén): is Water element and timely is at North Kan 1 Palace. It represents family, recuperate, relax living, public servant, administrative staff.

生门 (Shēng Mén): is Earth element and timely is at NE Gen 8 Palace. It represents business transaction, profit, new residence, wealth luck.

伤门 (Shāng Mén): is Wood element and timely is at East Zhen 3 Palace. It represents all transportation, sports, indirect wealth, gambling and demand for debt.

杜门 (Dù Mén): is Wood element and timely is at SE Xun 4 Palace. It represents concealment, hiding direction, secret, hard to get through, troops, industrial injury, tax affair or police.

景门 (Jǐng Mén): is Fire element and timely is at South Li 9 Palace. It represents blood related calamity, gorgeous place (night club), dispute, examination paper, documents, tactics, management plan, certificates and receipts.

死门 (Sǐ Mén): is Earth element and timely is at SW Kun 2 Palace. It represents dead man, tomb, land, calamity and bad luck.

惊门 (Jīng Mén): is Metal element and timely is at West Dui 7 Palace. It represents dispute and scandal, law suit, lawyer and panic.

The full picture of Qi Men chart
伏吟 (Fú Yín) Chart

The following is a sample of Qi Men Dun Jia original position 伏吟 (Fú Yín) chart:

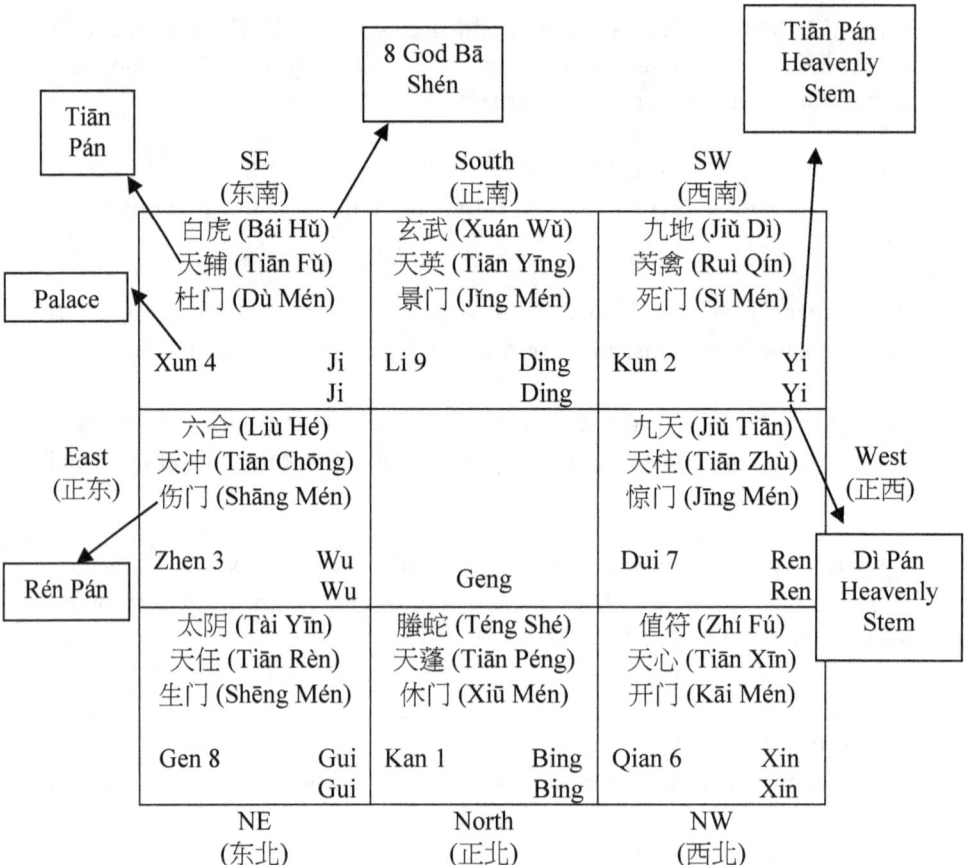

Note: 八神 (8 God - Bā Shén) has no original placement or 伏吟 (Fú Yín).

驿马星 (Traveling Horse - Yì Mǎ)

Yì Mǎ or Horse star as the name implies is like a horse, there will be movement or running away. Therefore in Qi Men Dun Jia, Yì Mǎ may indicate changes related to work, marriage or business.

The palace of Yì Mǎ is being determined as followed:

- Shen, Zi, Chen hour, Yì Mǎ star at Gen 8 Palace.
- Yin, Wu, Xu hour, Yì Mǎ star at Kun 2 Palace.
- Si, You, Chou hour, Yì Mǎ star at Qian 6 Palace.
- Hai, Mao, Wei hour, Yì Mǎ star at Xun 4 Palace.

巳 (Si) 巽四宫 (Xun 4) 辰 (Chen)	午 (Wu) 离九宫 Li 9	未 (Wei) 坤二宫 (Kun 2) 申 (Shen)
卯 (Mao) 震三宫 (Zhen 3)	中宫 (Middle 5)	酉 (You) 兑七宫 (Dui 7)
寅 (Yin) 马 艮八宫 (Gen 8) 丑 (Chou)	坎一宫 (Kan 1) 子 (Zi)	戌 (Xu) 乾六宫 (Qian 6) 亥 (Hai)

Shen – Zi – Chen Hour

巳 (Si) 巽四宫 (Xun 4) 辰 (Chen)	午 (Wu) 离九宫 Li 9	未 (Wei) 马 坤二宫 (Kun 2) 申 (Shen)
卯 (Mao) 震三宫 (Zhen 3)	中宫 (Middle 5)	酉 (You) 兑七宫 (Dui 7)
寅 (Yin) 艮八宫 (Gen 8) 丑 (Chou)	坎一宫 (Kan 1) 子 (Zi)	戌 (Xu) 乾六宫 (Qian 6) 亥 (Hai)

Yin – Wu – Xu Hour

巳 (Si) 巽四宮 (Xun 4) 辰 (Chen)	午 (Wu) 离九宮 Li 9	未 (Wei) 坤二宮 (Kun 2) 申 (Shen)
卯 (Mao) 震三宮 (Zhen 3)	中宮 (Middle 5)	酉 (You) 兑七宮 (Dui 7)
寅 (Yin) 艮八宮 (Gen 8) 丑 (Chou)	坎一宮 (Kan 1) 子 (Zi)	戌 (Xu) 马 乾六宮 (Qian 6) 亥 (Hai)

Si – You – Chou Hour

巳 (Si) 马 巽四宮 (Xun 4) 辰 (Chen)	午 (Wu) 离九宮 Li 9	未 (Wei) 坤二宮 (Kun 2) 申 (Shen)
卯 (Mao) 震三宮 (Zhen 3)	中宮 (Middle 5)	酉 (You) 兑七宮 (Dui 7)
寅 (Yin) 艮八宮 (Gen 8) 丑 (Chou)	坎一宮 (Kan 1) 子 (Zi)	戌 (Xu) 乾六宮 (Qian 6) 亥 (Hai)

Hai – Mao – Wei Hour

空 (Emptiness - Kōng)

Kōng means emptiness. In Qi Men Dun Jia, when the palace is in Kōng, it means the capability of the Shén (God), Mén (Door) and Xīng (Star) has only 20% capability. If it is auspicious; it only has 20% of auspiciousness. If it is inauspicious; it only has 20% of inauspiciousness. However, when the time arrived at the particular palace where it is in Kōng (空), the capability will be regained.

The method to determine Kōng is the same as the 60 Jia Zi 空亡 (Kōng Wáng – Death and Emptiness). The Kōng chart is together with Xún Shŏu.

旬首 (Leader - Xún Shǒu)

As the name Qi Men Dun Jia applied, "Dun Jia" means the Jia is hidden. So, in any Qi Men Dun Jia chart, "Jia" is hidden and the one that hide "Jia" is called Xún Shǒu or Leader. This information is needed when plotting Qi Men Dun Jia chart.

Xun	Jia Zi Xun	Jia Xu Xun	Jia Shen Xun	Jia Wu Xun	Jia Chen Xun	Jia Yin Xun
60 Jia Zi	甲(Jia) 子(Zi)	甲(Jia) 戌(Xu)	甲(Jia) 申(Shen)	甲(Jia) 午(Wu)	甲(Jia) 辰(Chen)	甲(Jia) 寅(Yin)
	乙(Yi) 丑(Chou)	乙(Yi) 亥(Hai)	乙(Yi) 酉(You)	乙(Yi) 未(Wei)	乙(Yi) 巳(Si)	乙(Yi) 卯(Mao)
	丙(Bing) 寅(Yin)	丙(Bing) 子(Zi)	丙(Bing) 戌(Xu)	丙(Bing) 申(Shen)	丙(Bing) 午(Wu)	丙(Bing) 辰(Chen)
	丁(Ding) 卯(Mao)	丁(Ding) 丑(Chou)	丁(Ding) 亥(Hai)	丁(Ding) 酉(You)	丁(Ding) 未(Wei)	丁(Ding) 巳(Si)
	戊(Wu) 辰(Chen)	戊(Wu) 寅(Yin)	戊(Wu) 子(Zi)	戊(Wu) 戌(Xu)	戊(Wu) 申(Shen)	戊(Wu) 午(Wu)
	己(Ji) 巳(Si)	己(Ji) 卯(Mao)	己(Ji) 丑(Chou)	己(Ji) 亥(Hai)	己(Ji) 酉(You)	己(Ji) 未(Wei)
	庚(Geng) 午(Wu)	庚(Geng) 辰(Chen)	庚(Geng) 寅(Yin)	庚(Geng) 子(Zi)	庚(Geng) 戌(Xu)	庚(Geng) 申(Shen)
	辛(Xin) 未(Wei)	辛(Xin) 巳(Si)	辛(Xin) 卯(Mao)	辛(Xin) 丑(Chou)	辛(Xin) 亥(Hai)	辛(Xin) 酉(You)
	壬(Ren) 申(Shen)	壬(Ren) 午(Wu)	壬(Ren) 辰(Chen)	壬(Ren) 寅(Yin)	壬(Ren) 子(Zi)	壬(Ren) 戌(Xu)
	癸(Gui) 酉(You)	癸(Gui) 未(Wei)	癸(Gui) 巳(Si)	癸(Gui) 卯(Mao)	癸(Gui) 丑(Chou)	癸(Gui) 亥(Hai)
空亡 (Kōng Wáng)	戌(Xu), 亥(Hai)	申(Shen), 酉(You)	午(Wu), 未(Wei)	辰(Chen), 巳(Si)	寅(Yin), 卯(Mao)	子(Zi), 丑(Chou)
旬首 (Xún Shǒu)	戊(Wu)	己(Ji)	庚(Geng)	辛(Xin)	壬(Ren)	癸(Gui)

In the chart above, for Jia Zi, Yi Chou, Bing Yin ... Gui You, Kōng is at Xu and Hai. For Jia Xu, Yi Hai, Bing Zi...Gui Wei, Kōng is at Shen and You.

In addition, for Jia Zi, Yi Chou, Bing Yin ... Gui You, 旬首 (Leader) is at Wu. For Jia Xu, Yi Hai, Bing Zi...Gui Wei, 旬首 (Leader) is at Ji.

In Qi Men Dun Jia there is Internal Pan and External Pan.

Below is a Yang Dun chart:

巳 (Si) 巽四宮 (Xun 4) 辰 (Chen)	午(Wu) 离九宮 Li 9	未 (Wei) 坤二宮 (Kun 2) 申 (Shen)
卯 (Mao) 震三宮 (Zhen 3)	中宮 (Middle 5) Yang Dun Chart	酉 (You) 兌七宮 (Dui 7)
寅 (Yin) 艮八宮 (Gen 8) 丑 (Chou)	坎一宮 (Kan 1) 子(Zi)	戌 (Xu) 乾六宮 (Qian 6) 亥 (Hai)

Kan 1, Gen 8, Zhen 3 and Xun 4 = Internal Pan

Li 9, Kun 2, Dui 7 and Qian 6 = External Pan

Below is a Yin Dun chart:

巳 (Si) 巽四宮 (Xun 4) 辰 (Chen)	午 (Wu) 离九宮 Li 9	未 (Wei) 坤二宮 (Kun 2) 申 (Shen)
卯 (Mao) 震三宮 (Zhen 3)	中宮 (Middle 5) Yin Dun Chart	酉 (You) 兌七宮 (Dui 7)
寅 (Yin) 艮八宮 (Gen 8) 丑 (Chou)	坎一宮 (Kan 1) 子 (Zi)	戌 (Xu) 乾六宮 (Qian 6) 亥 (Hai)

Kan 1, Gen 8, Zhen 3 and Xun 4 = External Pan

Li 9, Kun 2, Dui 7 and Qian 6 = Internal Pan

Qi Men Dun Jia Chart Plotting

Qi Men Dun Jia Season

To plot a Qi Men Dun Jia chart, you need to find out the season. A whole year is divided into 2 seasons and it is called Yang Dun (阳遁) and Yin Dun (阴遁). Depending on which technique is used, Yang Dun starts from Winter Solstice (冬至 - Dōng Zhì) up to Summer Solstice (夏至 - Xià Zhì). Yin Dun starts from Summer Solstice (夏至 - Xià Zhì) to Winter Solstice (冬至 - Dōng Zhì). There are a total of 9 types to each and they are called Ju (局). So, Yang Dun has 9 Ju and Yin Dun has 9 Ju. Each Ju is further categorized by Jia Zi hour (for Hour Qi Men Dun Jia). There are 60 Jia Zi hours and each Ju has 60 charts. As such, Yang Dun will have 9 X 60 = 540 charts. That's the same for Yin Dun, which gives a total of 1080 charts.

Month	二十四节气 (24 sub season - Er Shí Sì Jié Qì)	Start Date	Dun
First month (Yin)	立春 (Beginning of Spring - Lì Chūn), 雨水 (Rain Water - Yǔ Shuǐ)	Feb 4, 5 Feb 18, 19	Yang
2nd Month (Mao)	惊蛰 (Insect Awakening - Jīng Zhé), 春分 (Spring Equinox - Chūn Fēn)	Mar 5, 6 Mar 20, 21	Yang
3rd Month (Chen)	清明 (Pure Brightness - Qīng Míng), 谷雨 (Grain Rain - Gǔ Yǔ)	Apr 4, 5 Apr 20, 21	Yang
4th Month (Si)	立夏 (Beginning of Summer - Lì Xià), 小满 (Small Grain - Xiǎo Mǎn)	May 5, 6 May 21, 22	Yang
5th Month (Wu)	芒种 (Summer Harvest - Máng Zhòng), 夏至 (Summer Solstice - Xià Zhì)	Jun 5, 6 Jun 21, 22	Yang Yin
6th Month (Wei)	小署 (Mild Summer - Xiǎo Shǔ), 大署 (Extreme Summer - Dà Shǔ)	July 7, 8 July 22, 23	Yin
7th Month (Shen)	立秋 (Beginning of Autumn - Lì Qiū), 外署 (Outer Heat - Wài Shǔ)	Aug 7, 8 Aug 23, 24	Yin
8th Month (You)	白露 (White Dew - Bái Lù), 秋分 (Autumn Equinox - Qiū Fēn)	Sep 7, 8 Sep 23, 24	Yin
9th Month (Xu)	寒露 (Cold Dew - Hán Lù), 霜降 (Frost - Shuāng Jiàng)	Oct 8, 9 Oct 23, 24	Yin
10th Month (Hai)	立冬 (Beginning of Winter - Lì Dōng), 小雪 (Mild Snow - Xiǎo Xuě)	Nov 7, 8 Nov 22, 23	Yin
11th Month (Zi)	大雪 (Extreme Snow - Dà Xuě), 冬至 (Winter Solstice - Dōng Zhì)	Dec 7, 8 Dec 21, 22	Yin Yang
12th Month (Chou)	小寒 (Mild Cold - Xiǎo Hán), 大寒 (Extreme Cold - Dà Hán)	Jan 5, 6 Jan 20, 21	Yang

Steps to plot Qi Men Dun Jia chart

The Steps to plot a Qi Men Dun Jia chart is as follow:

1. Determine the Dun (Yang or Yin)
2. Use the Dun to determine the Ju
3. Determine the Xun Shou (旬首)
4. From the Ju, plot the Di Pan Heavenly Stem
5. From Di Pan plot the Tian Pan Heavenly Stem
6. Plot the 八神 (8 God - Bā Shén)
7. Plot the Tian Pan –九星 (Jiǔ Xīng)
8. Plot the Ren Pan -八门 (Bā Mén)

拆布 (Chāi Bù) Method of Plotting Qi Men Dun Jia Chart

1. Determine the Dun

In the Chāi Bù Method, the Qi Men Dun Jia season is determined as follow:

- Yang Dun is from 冬至 (Winter Solstice - Dōng Zhì) to 夏至 (Summer Solstice - Xià Zhì). Around 22nd Dec – 21st June.
- Yin Dun is from 夏至 (Summer Solstice - Xià Zhì) to 冬至 (Winter Solstice - Dōng Zhì). Around 22nd June – 21st Dec.

Use a reliable Thousand Year Calendar to find out when is the start of Winter or Summer Solstice.

2. Determine the Ju number

The Ju number depends heavily on the 24-subseason. That means if a day falls on a sub-season, there will be 2 different Ju number on the same day. If it falls on Winter Solstice or Summer Solstice, then the Dun change from Yang to Yin as well. Always refer to the Thousand Year Calendar to determine the 24-subseason before you continue. The sub-season Ju number chart is as follow:

Season	Ju#	Season	Ju#	Season	Ju#
芒种 (Máng Zhòng)	6 3 9	夏至 (Xià Zhì)	9 3 6	立秋 (Lì Qiū)	2 5 8
小满 (Xiǎo Mǎn)	5 2 8	小署 (Xiǎo Shǔ)	8 2 5	外署 (Wài Shǔ)	1 4 7
立夏 (Lì Xià)	4 1 7	大署 (Dà Shǔ)	7 1 4	白露 (Bái Lù)	9 3 6
Xun 4		Li 9		Kun 2	
Season	Ju#	中宮		Season	Ju#
谷雨 (Gǔ Yǔ)	5 2 8			秋分 (Qiū Fēn)	7 1 4
清明 (Qīng Míng)	4 1 7			寒露 (Hán Lù)	6 9 3
春分 (Chūn Fēn)	3 9 6			霜降 (Shuāng Jiàng)	5 8 2
Zhen 3				Dui 7	
Season	Ju#	Season	Ju#	Season	Ju#
立春 (Lì Chūn)	8 5 2	大寒 (Dà Hán)	3 9 6	立冬 (Lì Dōng)	6 9 3
雨水 (Yǔ Shuǐ)	9 6 3	小寒 (Xiǎo Hán)	2 8 5	小雪 (Xiǎo Xuě)	5 8 2
惊蛰 (Jīng Zhé)	1 7 4	冬至 (Dōng Zhì)	1 7 4	大雪 (Dà Xuě)	4 7 1
Gen 8		Kan 1		Qian 6	

The following conditions are used to determine the Ju#:

- Every sub-season is 15 days, every 5 days is 1 Unit, therefore, every sub-season is divided into Upper, Middle and Lower Unit.
- For example: 冬至 (Winter Solstice - Dōng Zhì) is 1, 7 and 4. 1 = Upper Unit, 7 = Middle Unit and 4 = Lower Unit.
- The Ju# is determine in rotation manner as long as it is within the sub-season. 1 -> 7 -> 4 -> 1 etc.
- Every 5 days, skip to the next Ju# within the sub-season.
- If the day is Jia (甲) or Ji (己), skip to the next Ju# within the sub-season.
- When transition from 1 sub-season to another, the Ju# is determine by whether the current Ju# is in Upper, Middle or Lower Unit. For example, if current sub-season is 大雪 (Extreme Snow - Dà Xuě) Ju# 1 (Lower Unit), when move to Winter Solstice 冬至 (Winter Solstice - Dōng Zhì), the Ju# is 4 (Lower Unit)
- If the 符头 (Fú Tóu) the leader Earthly Branches is Zi, Wu, Mao or You then use the Upper Unit.
- If the 符头 (Fú Tóu) the leader Earthly Branches is Yin, Shen, Si or Hai then use the Middle Unit.
- If the 符头 (Fú Tóu) the leader Earthly Branches is Chen, Xu, Chou or Wei then use the Lower Unit.

Example:

Date	Day	Sub-Season	Dun	Ju#	Unit
21/Dec/2010	Yi Si	大雪 (Extreme Snow - Dà Xuě)	Yin	1	Lower
22/Dec/2010	Bing Wu	冬至 (Winter Solstice - Dōng Zhì)	Yin Yang[4]	1 4	Lower
24/Dec/2010	Wu Shen	冬至 (Winter Solstice - Dōng Zhì)	Yang	4	Lower
25/Dec/2010	Ji You	冬至 (Winter Solstice - Dōng Zhì)	Yang	1[5]	Upper
30/Dec/2010	Jia Yin	冬至 (Winter Solstice - Dōng Zhì)	Yang	7[6]	Middle
04/Jan/2011	Ji Wei	冬至 (Winter Solstice - Dōng Zhì)	Yang	4	Lower
06/Jan/2011	Xin You	小寒 (Mild Cold - Xiǎo Hán)	Yang	5	Lower
09/Jan/2011	Jia Zi	小寒 (Mild Cold - Xiǎo Hán)	Yang	2	Upper
14/Jan/2011	Ji Si	小寒 (Mild Cold - Xiǎo Hán)	Yang	8	Middle

---

[4] After 冬至 (Dōng Zhì) is Yang

[5] Day is Ji

[6] After 5 days and Day is Jia

3. Determine the 旬首 (Xún Shǒu)

The 旬首 (Xún Shǒu) reference is as follow:

Xun	Jia Zi Xun	Jia Xu Xun	Jia Shen Xun	Jia Wu Xun	Jia Chen Xun	Jia Yin Xun
60 Jia Zi	甲(Jia) 子(Zi)	甲(Jia) 戌(Xu)	甲(Jia) 申(Shen)	甲(Jia) 午(Wu)	甲(Jia) 辰(Chen)	甲(Jia) 寅(Yin)
	乙(Yi) 丑(Chou)	乙(Yi) 亥(Hai)	乙(Yi) 酉(You)	乙(Yi) 未(Wei)	乙(Yi) 巳(Si)	乙(Yi) 卯(Mao)
	丙(Bing) 寅(Yin)	丙(Bing) 子(Zi)	丙(Bing) 戌(Xu)	丙(Bing) 申(Shen)	丙(Bing) 午(Wu)	丙(Bing) 辰(Chen)
	丁(Ding) 卯(Mao)	丁(Ding) 丑(Chou)	丁(Ding) 亥(Hai)	丁(Ding) 酉(You)	丁(Ding) 未(Wei)	丁(Ding) 巳(Si)
	戊(Wu) 辰(Chen)	戊(Wu) 寅(Yin)	戊(Wu) 子(Zi)	戊(Wu) 戌(Xu)	戊(Wu) 申(Shen)	戊(Wu) 午(Wu)
	己(Ji) 巳(Si)	己(Ji) 卯(Mao)	己(Ji) 丑(Chou)	己(Ji) 亥(Hai)	己(Ji) 酉(You)	己(Ji) 未(Wei)
	庚(Geng) 午(Wu)	庚(Geng) 辰(Chen)	庚(Geng) 寅(Yin)	庚(Geng) 子(Zi)	庚(Geng) 戌(Xu)	庚(Geng) 申(Shen)
	辛(Xin) 未(Wei)	辛(Xin) 巳(Si)	辛(Xin) 卯(Mao)	辛(Xin) 丑(Chou)	辛(Xin) 亥(Hai)	辛(Xin) 酉(You)
	壬(Ren) 申(Shen)	壬(Ren) 午(Wu)	壬(Ren) 辰(Chen)	壬(Ren) 寅(Yin)	壬(Ren) 子(Zi)	壬(Ren) 戌(Xu)
	癸(Gui) 酉(You)	癸(Gui) 未(Wei)	癸(Gui) 巳(Si)	癸(Gui) 卯(Mao)	癸(Gui) 丑(Chou)	癸(Gui) 亥(Hai)
旬首 (Xún Shǒu)	戊(Wu)	己(Ji)	庚(Geng)	辛(Xin)	壬(Ren)	癸(Gui)

The Xun Shou is determined by using the Hour. For example, 24th Dec 2010 at Wu Wu Hour is Yang Dun #4. Hence, It is under the Jia Yin Xun and therefore <u>Xun Shou is Gui</u>.

4. From the Ju plot the Di Pan Heavenly Stem

- Identify the Dun Ju based on the day (Yin or Yang Dun Ju #)
- Yang Dun fly forward, Ying Dun fly backward using Luo Shu sequence by making reference using the Ju # and Palace.
- E.g. if Yang Dun #4, then fly forward with the following sequence: Wu, Ji, Geng, Xin, Ren, Gui, Ding, Bing, Yi from Xun 4 palace. (Dun #4, so start from Xun 4 Palace)

4 (Wu)	Gui	Bing
Yi	Ji	Xin
Ren	Ding	Geng

- Note: if fly to middle palace, always move the Heavenly Stem to Kun 2 Palace.

- Yang Dun Di Pan Heavenly Stem:

Yang 1 Ju
Xin	Yi	Ji
Geng	Ren	Ding
Bing	1(Wu)	Gui

Yang 2 Ju
Geng	Bing	2(Wu)
Ji	Xin	Gui
Ding	Yi	Ren

Yang 3 Ju
Ji	Ding	Yi
3(Wu)	Geng	Ren
Gui	Bing	Xin

Yang 4 Ju
4(Wu)	Gui	Bing
Yi	Ji	Xin
Ren	Ding	Geng

Yang 5 Ju
Yi	Ren	Ding
Bing	5(Wu)	Geng
Xin	Gui	Ji

Yang 6 Ju
Bing	Xin	Gui
Ding	Yi	Ji
Geng	Ren	6(Wu)

Yang 7 Ju
Ding	Geng	Ren
Gui	Bing	7(Wu)
Ji	Xin	Yi

Yang 8 Ju
Gui	Ji	Xin
Ren	Ding	Yi
8(Wu)	Geng	Bing

Yang 9 Ju
Ren	9(Wu)	Geng
Xin	Gui	Bing
Yi	Ji	Ding

- Yin Dun Di Pan Heavenly Stem:

Yin 1 Ju
Ding	Ji	Yi
Bing	Gui	Xin
Geng	1(Wu)	Ren

Yin 2 Ju
Bing	Geng	2(Wu)
Yi	Ding	Ren
Xin	Ji	Gui

Yin 3 Ju
Yi	Xin	Ji
3(Wu)	Bing	Gui
Ren	Geng	Ding

Yin 4 Ju
4(Wu)	Ren	Geng
Ji	Yi	Ding
Gui	Xin	Bing

Yin 5 Ju
Ji	Gui	Xin
Geng	5(Wu)	Bing
Ding	Ren	Yi

Yin 6 Ju
Geng	Ding	Ren
Xin	Ji	Yi
Bing	Gyi	6(Wu)

Yin 7 Ju
Xin	Bing	Gui
Ren	Geng	7(Wu)
Yi	Ding	Ji

Yin 8 Ju
Ren	Yi	Ding
Gui	Xin	Ji
8(Wu)	Bing	Geng

Yin 9 Ju
Gui	9(Wu)	Bing
Ding	Ren	Geng
Ji	Yi	Xin

5. *From Di Pan plot the Tian Pan Heavenly Stem*

- Based on 旬首 (Xún Shǒu), Hour Heavenly Stem and Di Pan, use it to fly the Tian Pan Heavenly Stem.
- The 旬首 (Xún Shǒu) at Di Pan become the Tian Pan Heavenly Stem of Hour Heavenly Stem.
- For example:
    o Wu Wu Hour, <u>Xun Shou is Gui</u>.
    o Yang Dun #4
    o Gui from Di Pan is being rotate to Tian Pan where Wu (Hour Stem) is at Di Pan. (i.e. Xun 4 Palace)
    o Then follow by Bing Di Pan at Kun 2 to Li 9
    o Xin Di Pan at Dui 7 to Kun 2 etc

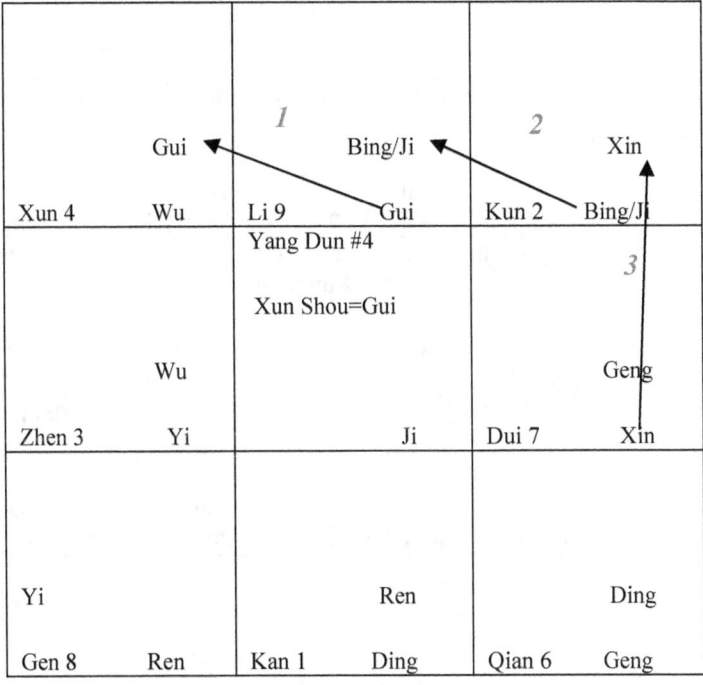

6. **Plot the** 八神 *(8 God - Bā Shén)*

- 值符 (Zhí Fú) always follow the Hour Stems in Di Pan.
- For Yang Dun: in <u>clockwise pattern</u>, put in 值符 (Zhí Fú), 螣蛇 (Téng Shé), 太阴 (Tài Yīn), 六合 (Liù Hé), 白虎 (Bái Hǔ), 玄武 (Xuán Wǔ), 九地 (Jiǔ Dì), 九天 (Jiǔ Tiān).
- For Yin Dun: in <u>anti-clockwise pattern</u>, put in 值符 (Zhí Fú), 螣蛇 (Téng Shé), 太阴 (Tài Yīn), 六合 (Liù Hé), 白虎 (Bái Hǔ), 玄武 (Xuán Wǔ), 九地 (Jiǔ Dì), 九天 (Jiǔ Tiān).
- From the above example, the Hour Stems is Wu Wu and Wu in Di Pan is at Xun 4 Palace. So, 值符 (Zhí Fú) is at Xun 4 Palace. From Xun 4 Palace, in clockwise pattern, put in 值符 (Zhí Fú), 螣蛇 (Téng Shé), etc.

值符 (Zhí Fú)	螣蛇 (Téng Shé)	太阴 (Tài Yīn)
Gui Xun 4 Wu	Bing/Ji Li 9 Gui	Xin Kun 2 Bing/Ji
九天 (Jiǔ Tiān)	Yang Dun #4 Xun Shou=Gui	六合 (Liù Hé)
Wu Zhen 3 Yi		Geng Dui 7 Xin
九地 (Jiǔ Dì)	玄武 (Xuán Wǔ)	白虎 (Bái Hǔ)
Yi Gen 8 Ren	Ren Kan 1 Ding	Ding Qian 6 Geng

- Yang Dun 八神 (8 God - Bā Shén) Fú Yín chart (original position) is as follow:

六合 (Liù Hé) Xun 4 Palace	白虎 (Bái Hǔ) Li 9 Palace	玄武 (Xuán Wǔ) Kun 2 Palace
太阴 (Tài Yīn) Zhen 3 Palace		九地 (Jiǔ Dì) Dui 7 Palace
螣蛇 (Téng Shé) Gen 8 Palace	值符 (Zhí Fú) Kan 1 Palace	九天 (Jiǔ Tiān) Qian 6 palace

- Yin Dun 八神 (8 God - Bā Shén) Fú Yín chart is as follow:

玄武 (Xuán Wǔ) Xun 4 Palace	白虎 (Bái Hǔ) Li 9 Palace	六合 (Liù Hé) Kun 2 Palace
九地 (Jiǔ Dì) Zhen 3 Palace		太阴 (Tài Yīn) Dui 7 Palace
九天 (Jiǔ Tiān) Gen 8 Palace	值符 (Zhí Fú) Kan 1 Palace	螣蛇 (Téng Shé) Qian 6 palace

7. Plot the Tian Pan – 九星 (Jiǔ Xīng)

- The Fú Yín Pan (original chart) for 九星 (Jiǔ Xīng) is as follow:

天辅 (Tiān Fǔ)	天英 (Tiān Yīng)	天芮 (Tiān Ruì)
Xun 4 Palace	Li 9 Palace	Kun 2 Palace
天冲 (Tiān Chōng)	天禽 (Tiān Qín)	天柱 (Tiān Zhù)
Zhen 3 Palace		Dui 7 Palace
天任 (Tiān Rèn)	天蓬 (Tiān Péng)	天心 (Tiān Xīn)
Gen 8 Palace	Kan 1 Palace	Qian 6 palace

- Note: 天禽 (Tiān Qín) will always follow 天芮 (Tiān Ruì)
- Determine the 直星 (leader of star - Zhí Xīng)
- Based on 旬首 (Xún Shǒu), find where it is in the Di Pan plotted chart.
- From the Di Pan, find out which palace it is in and mapped it back to the Fú Yín chart above, the star at that palace will follow 值符 (Zhí Fú).
- Plot in clockwise pattern starting from the 直星 (leader of star - Zhí Xīng)
- For example, Yang Dun #4, Wu Wu Hour, Xun Shou is Gui,
    o 值符 (Zhí Fú) is Xun 4 Palace.
    o Gui Di Pan is at Li 9 Palace.
    o Li 9 Palace is 天英 (Tiān Yīng) at original position. So 直星 (leader of star - Zhí Xīng) is 天英 (Tiān Yīng)
    o So put 天英 (Tiān Yīng) at Xun 4, following 值符 (Zhí Fú), 天芮 (Tiān Ruì) at Li 9 in clockwise pattern etc

值符 (Zhí Fú) 天英 (Tiān Yīng) Xun 4　　　　Gui 　　　　　　Wu	螣蛇 (Téng Shé) 芮禽 (Ruì Qín) 　　　　　Bing/Ji Li 9　　　　Gui	太阴 (Tài Yīn) 天柱 (Tiān Zhù) 　　　　　Xin Kun 2　　　Bing/Ji
九天 (Jiǔ Tiān) 天辅 (Tiān Fǔ) 　　　　　Wu Zhen 3　　　Yi	Yang Dun #4 Xun Shou=Gui	六合 (Liù Hé) 天心 (Tiān Xīn) 　　　　　Geng Dui 7　　　Xin
九地 (Jiǔ Dì) 天冲 (Tiān Chōng) 　　　　　Yi Gen 8　　　Ren	玄武 (Xuán Wǔ) 天任 (Tiān Rèn) 　　　　　Ren Kan 1　　　Ding	白虎 (Bái Hǔ) 天蓬 (Tiān Péng) 　　　　　Ding Qian 6　　　Geng

8. Plot the Ren Pan - 八门 (Bā Mén)

- The Fú Yín Pan (original chart) for 八门 (Bā Mén) is as follow:

杜门 (Dù Mén) Xun 4 Palace	景门 (Jǐng Mén) Li 9 Palace	死门 (Sǐ Mén) Kun 2 Palace
伤门 (Shāng Mén) Zhen 3 Palace		惊门 (Jīng Mén) Dui 7 Palace
生门 (Shēng Mén) Gen 8 Palace	休门 (Xiū Mén) Kan 1 Palace	开门 (Kāi Mén) Qian 6 palace

- From the plotted chart, find out which palace 值符 (Zhí Fú) is and what is the 九星 (Jiǔ Xīng).
- Based on the 九星 (Jiǔ Xīng), find out which palace it is in on the Fú Yín Chart:

天辅 (Tiān Fǔ)	天英 (Tiān Yīng)	天芮 (Tiān Ruì)
Xun 4 Palace	Li 9 Palace	Kun 2 Palace
天冲(Tiān Chōng)	天禽 (Tiān Qín)	天柱 (Tiān Zhù)
Zhen 3 Palace		Dui 7 Palace
天任 (Tiān Rèn)	天蓬(Tiān Péng)	天心 (Tiān Xīn)
Gen 8 Palace	Kan 1 Palace	Qian 6 palace

- From the palace find the 八门 (Bā Mén) in the 八门 (Bā Mén) Fú Yín Chart. That is the 直门 (leader of Mén (Door) - Zhí Mén)
- From the palace, if Yang Dun fly forward from the Xun to the hour. If Yin Dun fly backward from the Xun to the hour from the Xun.

Xun	Jia Zi Xun	Jia Xu Xun	Jia Shen Xun	Jia Wu Xun	Jia Chen Xun	Jia Yin Xun
60 Jia Zi	甲(Jia) 子(Zi)	甲(Jia) 戌(Xu)	甲(Jia) 申(Shen)	甲(Jia) 午(Wu)	甲(Jia) 辰(Chen)	甲(Jia) 寅(Yin)
	乙(Yi) 丑(Chou)	乙(Yi) 亥(Hai)	乙(Yi) 酉(You)	乙(Yi) 未(Wei)	乙(Yi) 巳(Si)	乙(Yi) 卯(Mao)
	丙(Bing) 寅(Yin)	丙(Bing) 子(Zi)	丙(Bing) 戌(Xu)	丙(Bing) 申(Shen)	丙(Bing) 午(Wu)	丙(Bing) 辰(Chen)
	丁(Ding) 卯(Mao)	丁(Ding) 丑(Chou)	丁(Ding) 亥(Hai)	丁(Ding) 酉(You)	丁(Ding) 未(Wei)	丁(Ding) 巳(Si)
	戊(Wu) 辰(Chen)	戊(Wu) 寅(Yin)	戊(Wu) 子(Zi)	戊(Wu) 戌(Xu)	戊(Wu) 申(Shen)	戊(Wu) 午(Wu)
	己(Ji) 巳(Si)	己(Ji) 卯(Mao)	己(Ji) 丑(Chou)	己(Ji) 亥(Hai)	己(Ji) 酉(You)	己(Ji) 未(Wei)
	庚(Geng) 午(Wu)	庚(Geng) 辰(Chen)	庚(Geng) 寅(Yin)	庚(Geng) 子(Zi)	庚(Geng) 戌(Xu)	庚(Geng) 申(Shen)
	辛(Xin) 未(Wei)	辛(Xin) 巳(Si)	辛(Xin) 卯(Mao)	辛(Xin) 丑(Chou)	辛(Xin) 亥(Hai)	辛(Xin) 酉(You)
	壬(Ren) 申(Shen)	壬(Ren) 午(Wu)	壬(Ren) 辰(Chen)	壬(Ren) 寅(Yin)	壬(Ren) 子(Zi)	壬(Ren) 戌(Xu)
	癸(Gui) 酉(You)	癸(Gui) 未(Wei)	癸(Gui) 巳(Si)	癸(Gui) 卯(Mao)	癸(Gui) 丑(Chou)	癸(Gui) 亥(Hai)
旬首 (Xún Shǒu)	戊(Wu)	己(Ji)	庚(Geng)	辛(Xin)	壬(Ren)	癸(Gui)

- From the example, Yang Dun #4, Wu Wu Hour, Xun Shou is Gui under the Jia Yin Xun.
    - 值符 (Zhí Fú) is Xun 4 Palace.
    - 直星 (leader of star - Zhí Xīng) is 天英 (Tiān Yīng)
    - 天英 (Tiān Yīng) is originally at Li 9 Palace in the Fú Yín chart.
    - Li 9 Palace is 景门 (Jǐng Mén) in the 八门 (Bā Mén) Fú Yín chart.
    - The 直门 (leader of Mén (Door) - Zhí Mén) is 景门 (Jǐng Mén).
    - Xun Shou is Gui, at Di Pan Li 9 Palace. Since it is Yang Dun, fly forward with Luo Shu pattern using the Xun Shou Chart from Li 9 Palace starting from Jia Yin (Xun), Kan 1 = Yi Mao, Kun 2 = Bing Chen, Zhen 3 = Ding Si, Xun 4 =

Wu Wu (the hour). Put 景门 (Jǐng Mén) at Xun 4 Palace, 死门 (Sǐ Mén) at Li 9 Palace
- Note: if Yin Dun, then Li 9 = Jia Yin, Gen 8 = Yi Mao, Dui 7 = Bing Chen etc etc

值符 (Zhí Fú) 天英 (Tiān Yīng) 景门 (Jǐng Mén) 　　　　　Gui Xun 4　　　Wu	螣蛇 (Téng Shé) 芮禽 (Ruì Qín) 死门 (Sǐ Mén) 　　　　　Bing/Ji Li 9　　　Gui	太阴 (Tài Yīn) 天柱 (Tiān Zhù) 惊门 (Jīng Mén) 　　　　　Xin Kun 2　　　Bing/Ji
九天 (Jiǔ Tiān) 天辅 (Tiān Fǔ) 杜门 (Dù Mén) 　　　　　Wu Zhen 3　　　Yi	Yang Dun #4 Xun Shou=Gui	六合 (Liù Hé) 天心 (Tiān Xīn) 开门 (Kāi Mén) 　　　　　Geng Dui 7　　　Xin
九地 (Jiǔ Dì) 天冲 (Tiān Chōng) 伤门 (Shāng Mén) 　　　　　Yi Gen 8　　　Ren	玄武 (Xuán Wǔ) 天任 (Tiān Rèn) 生门 (Shēng Mén) 　　　　　Ren Kan 1　　　Ding	白虎 (Bái Hǔ) 天蓬 (Tiān Péng) 休门 (Xiū Mén) 　　　　　Ding Qian 6　　　Geng

9. 空 *(Emptiness - Kōng)*

- Indicate the 空 (Emptiness - Kōng).
- Use the Hour Stems as reference to find out which Earthly Branches is 空 (Emptiness - Kōng).
- The placement of Earthly Branches in Qi Men Dun Jia is as follow:

巳 (Si) Xun 4 辰 (Chen)	午 (Wu) Li 9	未 (Wei) Kun 2 申 (Shen)
卯 (Mao) Zhen 3	Middle 5	酉 (You) Dui 7
寅 (Yin) Gen 8 丑 (Chou)	Kan 1 子 (Zi)	戌 (Xu) Qian 6 亥 (Hai)

Xun	Jia Zi Xun	Jia Xu Xun	Jia Shen Xun	Jia Wu Xun	Jia Chen Xun	Jia Yin Xun
60 Jia Zi	甲(Jia) 子(Zi)	甲(Jia) 戌(Xu)	甲(Jia) 申(Shen)	甲(Jia) 午(Wu)	甲(Jia) 辰(Chen)	甲(Jia) 寅(Yin)
	乙(Yi) 丑(Chou)	乙(Yi) 亥(Hai)	乙(Yi) 酉(You)	乙(Yi) 未(Wei)	乙(Yi) 巳(Si)	乙(Yi) 卯(Mao)
	丙(Bing) 寅(Yin)	丙(Bing) 子(Zi)	丙(Bing) 戌(Xu)	丙(Bing) 申(Shen)	丙(Bing) 午(Wu)	丙(Bing) 辰(Chen)
	丁(Ding) 卯(Mao)	丁(Ding) 丑(Chou)	丁(Ding) 亥(Hai)	丁(Ding) 酉(You)	丁(Ding) 未(Wei)	丁(Ding) 巳(Si)
	戊(Wu) 辰(Chen)	戊(Wu) 寅(Yin)	戊(Wu) 子(Zi)	戊(Wu) 戌(Xu)	戊(Wu) 申(Shen)	戊(Wu) 午(Wu)
	己(Ji) 巳(Si)	己(Ji) 卯(Mao)	己(Ji) 丑(Chou)	己(Ji) 亥(Hai)	己(Ji) 酉(You)	己(Ji) 未(Wei)
	庚(Geng) 午(Wu)	庚(Geng) 辰(Chen)	庚(Geng) 寅(Yin)	庚(Geng) 子(Zi)	庚(Geng) 戌(Xu)	庚(Geng) 申(Shen)
	辛(Xin) 未(Wei)	辛(Xin) 巳(Si)	辛(Xin) 卯(Mao)	辛(Xin) 丑(Chou)	辛(Xin) 亥(Hai)	辛(Xin) 酉(You)
	壬(Ren) 申(Shen)	壬(Ren) 午(Wu)	壬(Ren) 辰(Chen)	壬(Ren) 寅(Yin)	壬(Ren) 子(Zi)	壬(Ren) 戌(Xu)
	癸(Gui) 酉(You)	癸(Gui) 未(Wei)	癸(Gui) 巳(Si)	癸(Gui) 卯(Mao)	癸(Gui) 丑(Chou)	癸(Gui) 亥(Hai)
空亡 (Kōng Wáng)	戌(Xu), 亥(Hai)	申(Shen), 酉(You)	午(Wu), 未(Wei)	辰(Chen), 巳(Si)	寅(Yin), 卯(Mao)	子(Zi), 丑(Chou)

- From the example, Yang Dun #4, Wu Wu Hour, 空 (Emptiness - Kōng) is at Zi & Chou.

10. 驿马星 (Travelling Horse - Yì Mǎ)

- The palace of Yi Ma is being determined as followed:
    - Shen, Zi, Chen hour: Horse Star at Gen 8 Palace.
    - Yin, Wu, Xu hour: Horse Star at Kun 2 Palace.
    - Si, You, Chou hour: Horse Star at Qian 6 Palace.
    - Hai, Mao, Wei hour: Horse Star at Xun 4 Palace.
- From the example, Wu Wu Hour, the Horse Star is at Kun 2 Palace.
- The 拆布 (Chāi Bù) Chart for 24th Dec 2010 at Wu Wu Hour:

值符 (Zhí Fú) 天英 (Tiān Yīng) 景门 (Jǐng Mén) 　　　　　　Gui Xun 4　　　　Wu	螣蛇 (Téng Shé) 芮禽 (Ruì Qín) 死门 (Sǐ Mén) 　　　　Bing/Ji Li 9　　　　Gui	太阴 (Tài Yīn) 马 天柱 (Tiān Zhù) 惊门 (Jǐng Mén) 　　　　　　Xin Kun 2　　　Bing/Ji
九天 (Jiǔ Tiān) 天辅 (Tiān Fǔ) 杜门 (Dù Mén) 　　　　　　Wu Zhen 3　　　　Yi	Yang Dun #4 Xun Shou=Gui	六合 (Liù Hé) 天心 (Tiān Xīn) 开门 (Kāi Mén) 　　　　　　Geng Dui 7　　　　Xin
九地 (Jiǔ Dì)　O 天冲 (Tiān Chōng) 伤门 (Shāng Mén) 　　　　　　Yi Gen 8　　　　Ren	玄武 (Xuán Wǔ)　O 天任 (Tiān Rèn) 生门 (Shēng Mén) 　　　　　Ren Kan 1　　　Ding	白虎 (Bái Hǔ) 天蓬 (Tiān Péng) 休门 (Xiū Mén) 　　　　　Ding Qian 6　　　Geng

Usage of Qi Men Dun Jia

Qi Men Dun Jia Usage

Can you imagine Zhuge Liang won the Battle of Red Cliff by using Divination? I don't think so. From my understanding and what I have learnt, Qi Men Dun Jia can be used for:

- Divination
- Application
- Destiny Analysis
- Change Name
- Fengshui Prescription
- Religious Matter
- Personal Wellbeing

Divination

For those who had learnt Qi Men Dun Jia before, this is the most basic fundamental of Qi Men Dun Jia. You can use Qi Men Dun Jia Divination to forecast:

- Relationship Matters: divorce, 3rd party affair, scandal and legal entanglement.
- Wealth and Investment: status of current wealth, join venture, investment into business.
- Interview and Academic: whether the interview or exam will be successful.
- Accuracy of information: whether the person is lying or had provided fake information.
- Perform Fengshui audit and destiny analysis using divination.
- Mundane stuff like find lost items and weather forecast. My student even used it to find his wife whereabouts in the shopping mall.

Application

This is where the real deal of Qi Men Dun Jia comes in. This is basically choosing a good date or time and proper action to make things happen. This is where the concept of Heaven, Earth & Man (天时, 地利, 人和) comes in.

So, what can Qi Men Dun Jia do for you? There are 2 parts to this:

1. Based on the date or time used for certain endeavor, find out what is the possible problem or issue.
2. Choose a good date or time for important endeavor.

Please note that not many Qi Men masters are teaching this as this is regard as guarded secret and not to be easily revealed.

Marriage

For some married couples, certain (bad) things start to happen after marriage. This could be due to wrong date or time used. So, from the date and time chosen for marriage, we can use Qi Men Dun Jia to find out what is the problem or issue that had happened or will happen. For example, unable to conceive, 3rd party comes into the picture, divorce, sickness or even death.

For those who is going to get married, we can use Qi Men Dun Jia to choose a good date or time for marriage to ensure good results (e.g. kids or harmony)

House Renovation

Sometimes choosing a wrong date for house renovation can cause dire effect. Based on the date or time used, we can use Qi Men Dun Jia to find out what are the dire effects (e.g. injury at work, bankruptcy etc)

On the other hand, by using Qi Men Dun Jia to choose a good date or time for house renovation, we can ensure good returns (harmony, wealth etc).

Yin Fengshui

Sometimes the same type of calamity (e.g. same type of sickness) might befall on some of the family members after the burial of ancestor. This could be due to the wrong date or time being used for burial. Based on the wrong date or time used, the reasons of calamity and the affected family members can be determined by using Qi Men Dun Jia.

By using Qi Men Dun Jia, we can choose a good date or time for re-burial to ensure good blessing to descendants.

Move-in to new house

Bad things could happen if wrong date or time is used for move-in ceremony. There could be potential health issue, injury, loss of job, loss of wealth etc because of that. Based on the date or time used, all these effects can be derived by using Qi Men Dun Jia.

To ensure prosperity, good health and wealth, a good Qi Men Dun Jia date or time can be used for move-in ceremony.

Some masters brand the above techniques as Qi Men Dun Jia Fengshui but to me, this is just a simple divination based on the date or time used for move-in. A "real" Qi Men Dun Jia Fengshui involved using a person Qi Men Dun Jia Bazi to match to the person's house. This includes the direction of bed as well as the suitable colour scheme for the people staying in the house.

Opening Ceremony for Business

The key focus of business is to make money. If there are no customers patronizing, then it affects the profits. As such, choosing a good date or time for business opening is also as important. Choosing a wrong date or time for business opening has dire effect on the business.

For example, choosing a time where the hour is in "Kong" will result in poor customers' patronage. We can use Qi Men Dun Jia to choose a prosperous date or time for business opening, by factoring in business facing or sitting, owner's bazi and good date to optimize Heaven, Earth & Man effect (天时, 地利, 人和).

Interview or Exam

Finding a good job and passing an exam are important milestones for a person. Sometimes, going for interview or exam on the wrong date and time will cause failure in getting the job or unable to pass the exam. Therefore, choosing a good date or time is very important.

You can use Qi Men Dun Jia Divination to find out what are the chances of passing and based on that, use Qi Men Dun Jia Fengshui to re-mediate. Alternatively, you can choose a good date or time when going for interview or exam. Further supplement it by using Qi Men Dun Jia Fengshui technique to ensure optimum results.

Assemble of Bed

Qi Men Dun Jia has a built-in compass. Therefore, we can use it to "correct" certain condition. Assemble of bed is another method specially designed by my fore-masters to do such correction. Basically, prior to the date selected, dissemble the bed and leave the mattress up on the wall for at least 24 hours. At the specific date and time, re-assemble the bed to the correct direction.

The date and time chosen is to achieve the specific results that the person desire. For example, for those who are always sick can chose a date or time to improve health.

Other forms of application

You can use Qi Men Dun Jia to:

- Choose a good date or time to seek wealth to ensure good returns.
- Choose a good date or time for horse betting, 4D betting, casino gambling, asking favour from boss, negotiation, court hearing, filing of lawsuit etc.
- Based on current date and time, find a good direction or location to hide, escape (avoid being arrested).

Destiny Analysis

Qi Men Dun Jia can be used for destiny analysis. Like Zi Ping bazi or Zi Wei Dou Shou, you can use your birth date and time to plot the Qi Men Dun Jia chart. You can see pretty much the same things (or more) as in Zi Ping bazi.

Your Qi Men Dun Jia Bazi chart is basically like your life compass. It tells you:

- How good is your wealth, both direct and indirect wealth?
- How good is your relationship? For example, your relationship with spouse, kids, parents, siblings, boss, who are the people that will potentially sabotage you (小人), who are your noblemen etc.
- Major events that are happening to your spouse, kids, parents or siblings based on your Qi Men Dun Jia bazi.
- You can use it to choose a house that suit your bazi and use Qi Men Dun Jia Fengshui to further enhance it.
- Your health status and where are your weak organs. When will your sickness manifest.
- Your career; type of career that best suits you, relationship with your boss and the environment. The location of your office that suits your bazi.
- Business acumen; suitable to own a business or simply stay employed.
- The colour scheme that suits you based on your Qi Men Dun Jia Bazi.
- Sequences of events that are happening or going to happen in your entire life.
- Time of Death.

Change Name

The Chinese believed the following impacts a person life:

一命，二运，三风水，四积功德，五读书，六名，七相，八敬神，九交贵人，十养生.

Translated to:

1-Destiny, 2-Luck, 3-Fengshui, 4-Do good deed, 5-Education, 6-Name, 7-Appearance, 8-respect God, 9-networking, 10-Life cultivation.

So, a good name is ranked 6th in the hierarchy of influence. As such, based on your Qi Men Dun Jia Destiny chart, you can use Qi Men Dun Jia to change your name that compliment your Destiny chart and therefore enhanced your life.

Fengshui

I can use Qi Men Dun Jia divination to find out the Fengshui condition of your house without knowing where you stay and prescribe Qi Men Dun Jia Fengshui remedy to you based on the divination made. I can derive the condition or situation of the people living in the house without knowing their birth date or time.

Using your Qi Men Dun Jia Destiny chart, I will be able to tell the flaw in your chart and prescribe Qi Men Dun Jia Fengshui remedy for you. This is where Bazi does the diagnosis and Fengshui does the prescription.

Any flaws, issues and problems can be fixed using the bed dissemble or assemble method. For example, when a perfectly healthy couple failed to have children and there is nothing wrong with their bazi (according to Qi Men Dun Jia Destiny Analysis), the problem could be due to the wrong date being used during their wedding. Another example is that after moving into the new house, the husband lost his job and this is attributed to the wrong move-in date being used. So, by dissemble and reassemble the bed again on good Qi Men date or time, we can change a person's luck. I've helped my clients who were on the verge of bankruptcy by using this technique.

For those who are in dire state, we can use the Qi Men Dun Jia Life Changing method as well to turn the luck around (see Qi Men Dun Jia Life Changing Method).

Religious Matter

Last but not least, Qi Men Dun Jia can be used on spiritual or religious matter. There is Qi Men Dun Jia Talisman that can be used as remedy. Good date and time is selected to "bless" the Talisman to ensure the effectiveness. Qi Men Dun Jia Date Selection can be used to choose a good date and time to perform religious matter.

In addition, you can also choose a good date and time and sector for spiritual matters. This can be further enhanced by being at a good Fengshui place.

Your Qi Men Dun Jia Destiny chart can be used to read information about your past life(s). This is more related to the karma effect. Things happening in this life are related to what you did in your past life.

Qi Men Dun Jia Life Changing Method

Qi Men Life Changing Method (种生基)

In Qi Men Dun Jia, there is a technique that will help to change a person's life around. This technique is closely guarded and regards as the life buoy of a person in dire state. This Qi Men Life Changing Method can be used to turn around a bankrupt situation, improves one's health, improve husband and wife relationship or even turn around a dead-and-alive situation.

Not many masters know this technique as it requires the master to attain certain "Dao" (道) or certain level of enlightenment to perform this. This is a very dangerous technique and when used wrongly will cause bad effect on the master as well as the person's life that needs the change.

What is Qi Men Life Changing Method?

It is basically a technique that makes use of the aspect of Heaven, Earth and Man (天时地利人和). Heaven (天时) is about choosing a good date and time by using Hour Qi Men Dun Jia. Earth (地利) is basically about choosing a good Fengshui Place based on the purpose this person wants to achieve. Man (人和) is using this person's DNA to activate the combination of Heaven, Earth and Man and harness the energy of the universe using Qi Men Dun Jia and achieve the desire results.

For example, if a person is on the verge of bankruptcy, a good date and time need to be chosen to match the person's bazi. This is the Heaven aspect (天时). Next, a good place that usher wealth need to be chosen and this is known as the Earth aspect (地利). Lastly, the person's finger nails, hair, underwear and bazi will be placed in a box. The box will be buried in the chosen place at the chosen time. This is forms the Human aspect (人和). That's why this method is sometimes known as Life Grave (生墓).

This method is specially designed by all my fore-masters. For example, if you want to increase your wealth, your DNA will be planted in a place that increases wealth. It's like a fixed deposit in the bank. You deposit your DNA to collect monthly interest. There is no harm done to the bank and others. Likewise, it will not cause harm to the environment and other people. Like fixed deposit, you can also deposit your money in many banks to earn more interest. For Qi Men Life Changing Method, you can deposit your DNA in various good Fengshui environments to reap the good energy and earn "interest" from it.

Most of the methods being published were using graveyard to bury the DNA. However, the method that was passed down by my grandmasters does not necessary require a graveyard. We need a place that has good Fengshui for specific purpose. For example, to increase wealth, we need a place that has good Fengshui for wealth.

Divination vs Destiny

Divination and Destiny Reading

A lot of people asked me on how accurate are the divination and destiny reading. Some asked why destiny reading is so accurate when reading past events but not accurate in predicting the future. Mostly asked question was can we change our destiny?

Chinese has a saying: 人可信命但不可任命. It means, human can believe in destiny but can't leave it to destiny. Believing in destiny means to embrace what you have and work around its advantages and disadvantages. For example, if you are in bad luck, then stay low, do your preparation and wait for your good luck. When you are in good luck, then you should go all out. If you leave it to destiny, then you are basically doing nothing.

There was a story of a middle-income person that went for destiny analysis. He was told that he will be millionaire in 5 years' time. During the 5-years, he basically stays at home and waits for the time to come. He did nothing and became so sick and passed away. When he reached the other world, the chief investigator asked why he was here when his time was not up. According to his record, he was supposed to be rich so he asked the god of wealth why he didn't deliver the money to him. The gods of wealth replied that he was there and knock on the door but nobody answered. The person was so sick that he can't even open the door. So, the moral of the story is that when your time is up to be rich, you need to be physically capable to accept the wealth.

What is divination?

Dictionary.com defined divination as:

1. The practice of attempting to foretell future events or discover hidden knowledge by occult or supernatural means.
2. Augury; prophecy: *The divination of the high priest was fulfilled.*
3. Perception by intuition; instinctive foresight.

It is defined as "occult" or "supernatural" as it cannot be explained scientifically.

In Chinese Meta-Physics, divination provides a "peep" into future events. However, the actual outcome depends on many factors. Here are some of the possible scenarios:

1. The person asking, after knowing the result, did nothing about it.
2. The person asking, after knowing the result, reacts negatively about it.
3. The person asking, after knowing the result, decides to do something about it.

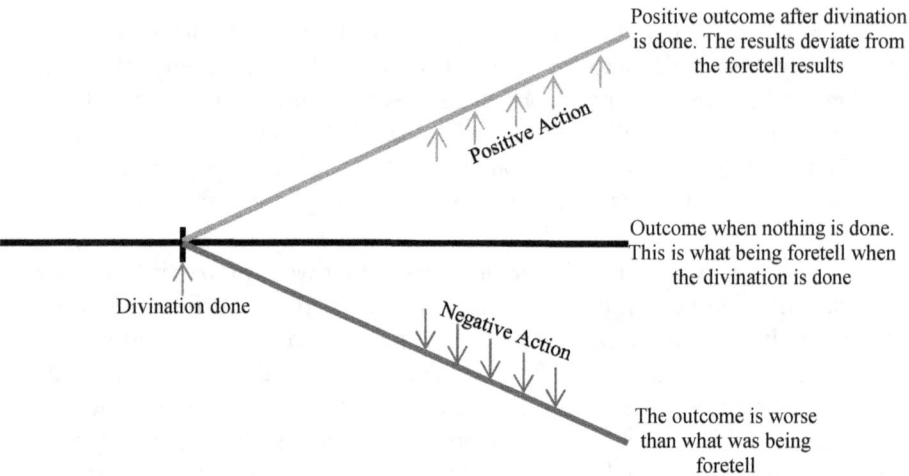

For example, a person came to ask about his marriage situation and the foretell outcome is that the person will divorce in 2 months' time. If he does nothing about it, then the outcome will come true in next 2 months. However, if he decided to salvage the relationship and does all he can to win back his wife, then the situation might change. (e.g. He can brings her for vacation for 2 months).

So, does it mean that the divination system is not accurate? Not really. It depends on many factors:

1. How a question is being asked and the background surrounding the question being asked (I will explain this later).
2. How the person reacts to the foretell results (as describe above).
3. Any unknown circumstances that might affects the outcome.

Why asking the correct question is important?

A friend of mine went for parent volunteer interview and asked me whether the interview will be successful. So, I plotted the chart and use the generic Day Stem to represent him. In the palace, there was Si Men and it was in restricting situation with Tian Fu, which represented the interviewer. Therefore, I told him that his interview is unsuccessful. A few days later, he informed me that he was selected. I was puzzled at first. He told me that the interview was a group interview where all parents were being interviewed at the same time. As such, using the generic Day Stem to represent him was incorrect as in this situation (group interview), Day Stem represents all the parents. So, when I use his birth year to represent him, I can then see the "correct" outcome from the plotted chart.

Lesson learnt; always find out the background and nature of the question asked before foretelling the outcome.

What are the unknown circumstances?

We only know what we know and we don't know what we don't know. Since it is unknown then there is no way we can find out. We can only react based on the information available. Like the example above, when the person take action, the outcome will be different from what's being foretell. Does this means that divination cannot be used anymore? The answer is No. We can always do another divination every time there is change in the circumstances (e.g. the person take action or new discovery)

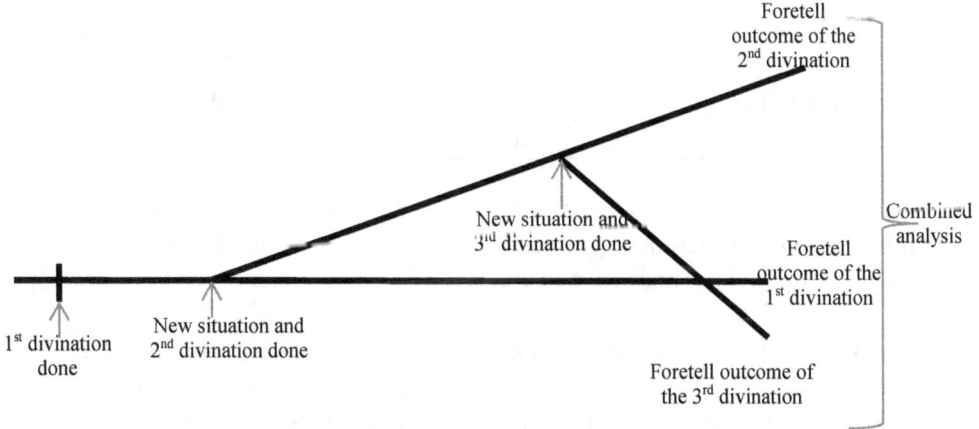

Isn't the above situation similar to what's going on with missing plane? Things will be changing rapidly.

Here is an example of how you can make use of the divination results to your advantage. This divination was done by one of my student. Her father complained about seeing double on his left eyes. She brought her father to see an eyes specialist, done some MRI but could not find anything wrong. So, she did a divination. Here is the chart:

Hour	Day	Month	Year
Gui	Yi	Ding	Jia
Wei	You	Mao	Wu

YangDun#7 Hour: **GuiWei** ; 直符(ZhíFú): **天任 (Tiān Rèn)** ; 直使(ZhíShǐ): **生门 (Shēng Mén)** ; 旬首(XúnShǒu): **JiaXuJi**		
螣蛇 (Téng Shé) 天冲 (Tiān Chōng) 杜门 (Dù Mén) Xun 4 Gui Ding	太阴 (Tài Yīn) 天辅 (Tiān Fǔ) 景门 (Jǐng Mén) Li 9 Ding Geng	六合 (Liù Hé) 天英 (Tiān Yīng) 死门 (Sǐ Mén) Kun 2 Geng Ren/Bing
值符 (Zhí Fú) 天任 (Tiān Rèn) 伤门 (Shāng Mén) Zhen 3 Ji Gui	YangDun#7 Hour: GuiWei ©Calvin Yap	白虎 (Bái Hǔ) 禽芮 (Qín Ruì) 惊门 (Jīng Mén) Dui 7 Ren/Bing Wu
九天 (Jiǔ Tiān) 天蓬 (Tiān Péng) 生门 (Shēng Mén) Gen 8 Xin Ji	九地 (Jiǔ Dì) 天心 (Tiān Xīn) 休门 (Xiū Mén) Kan 1 Yi Xin	玄武 (Xuán Wǔ) 天柱 (Tiān Zhù) 开门 (Kāi Mén) Qian 6 Wu Yi

From the chart, 天芮 (Tiān Ruì) sickness star is at Dui 7 Palace and there is no indication that there is anything wrong with his eyes. In addition, it is in Kong. So, the sickness cannot be detected.

One thing to note, the Hour Heavenly Stem Gui which is at Xun 4 Palace with 杜门 (Dù Mén) and 螣蛇 (Téng Shé). Therefore, matter asked will be stuck. So, asking about health matter, it will be stuck. She was in dilemma. 天心 (Tiān Xīn) represents doctor which is in Kan 1 Palace with 休门 (Xiū

Mén) and 九地 (Jiǔ Dì). 休门 (Xiū Mén) means the doctor is relaxed. 九地 (Jiǔ Dì) also means low or sub-standard. So, the doctor did not perform a thorough check on him.

Hence, I advised her to seek 2nd opinion on Bing, Ren or You day when the 天芮 (Tiān Ruì) is filled up.

On 15th April 2014, which is a Bing Chen day, she brought her father to see another doctor. Within 10 mins, the doctor diagnosed her father has border line diabetic and further blood test confirmed that. She told me that her in fact her father went to see another doctor and the doctor asked him to go for droopy eye lid surgery.

Instead of listening to the 2nd doctor and go for eye lid surgery, she decided to follow the chart and seek another doctor's opinion based on the information obtained from divination. They benefited from the divination system by reacting and using the information obtained from it. Does it mean that the divination is not correct as the chart showed that the sickness cannot be detected but it was confirmed that the problem is due to mild diabetic?

Destiny Reading

In the olden days, a person's life is graded as 富 (Fù) - Rich, 貴 (Guì) – Noble, 貧 (Pín) - Poor or 賤 (Jiàn) – Despicable. In ancient Chinese time, a Noble (貴) person might not be a Rich (富) person. Some wanted to remain poor and noble. However, the current modern societies, most of the Noble people are Rich and most of the Rich people can "buy" nobility. So, I put Rich and Noble in the same level:

富 (Fù) - Rich	貴 (Guì) - Noble
貧 (Pín) - Poor	
賤 (Jiàn) - Despicable	

The Poor are the people who need to work hard to earn a living. Of course, their only desire is to move up the chain to become Rich and Noble.

The Despicable are the slum dog, beggar, prostitutes, pimps and etc. They will do things that are abnormal or socially not acceptable by the society for a living.

So, does it mean that someone that is born with a Despicable life (as according to Destiny Analysis) will not be Rich and Noble? The answer is No.

There was a story about a blind female beggar in Saudi that has begged for 50 years died suddenly and left behind SR 3 Million in cash, jewellery, gold worth SR1 Million and four buildings.

(http://www.arabnews.com/news/541011)

Believing or leaving to Destiny

Chinese has a saying: 人可信命但不可任命 (Human can believe in destiny but can't leave it to destiny).

Believing in destiny means to embrace what you have and work around its advantages and disadvantages. For example, if you are in bad luck, then stay low, do your preparation and wait for your good luck. When you are in good luck, then you should go all out. If you leave it to destiny, then you are basically doing nothing to improve your life.

Confucius said: 不知命，无以为君子也 (Bù Zhī Mìng Wú Yǐ Wéi Jūn Zǐ Yě). People who don't understand Destiny, they are not gentlemen. Basically Confucius said that every human being needs to understand and act according to one's destiny. If not, how to become a gentleman?

Destiny – Luck cycle

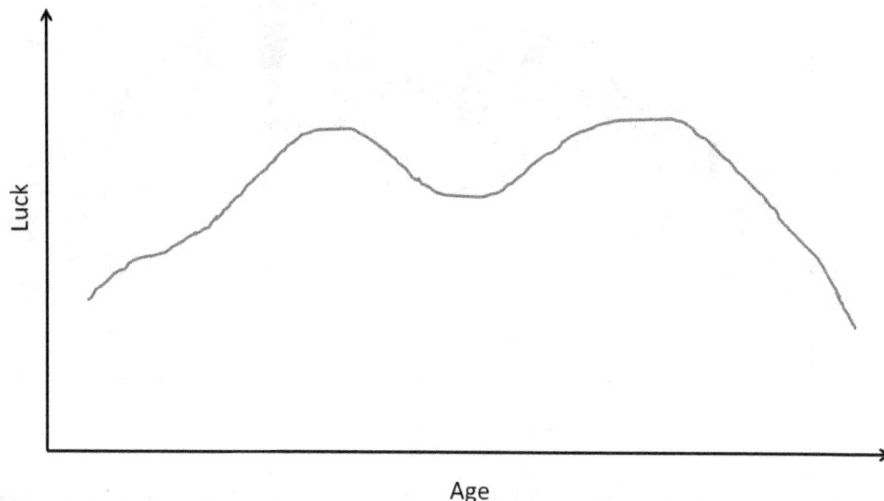

Everybody will go through ups and downs on certain time. This is called luck cycle and these will fluctuate throughout a person's life. In actual fact, a luck cycle is not a thin line like the diagram above:

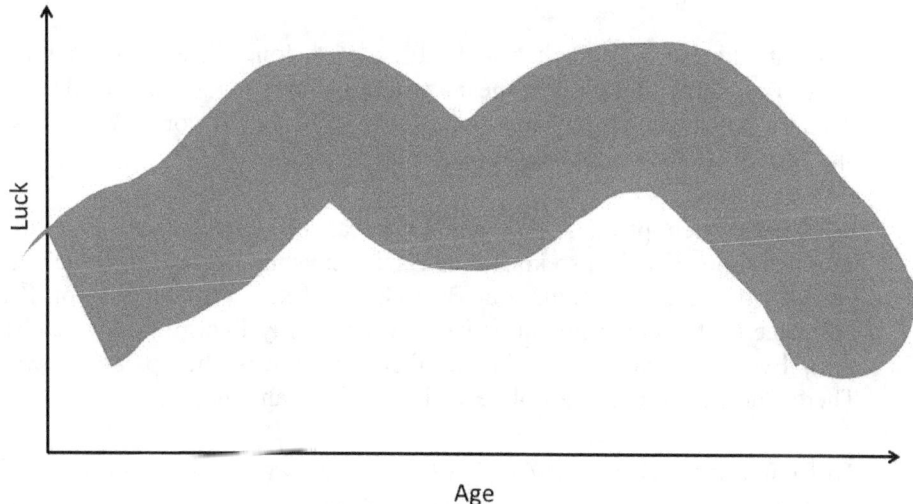

In reality, it is actually very thick. This will form a boundary of your luck within a given time. So, the key idea is to maximize your luck; regardless of whether it is down or up. You push it to the max to achieve optimum results as shown in the diagram below:

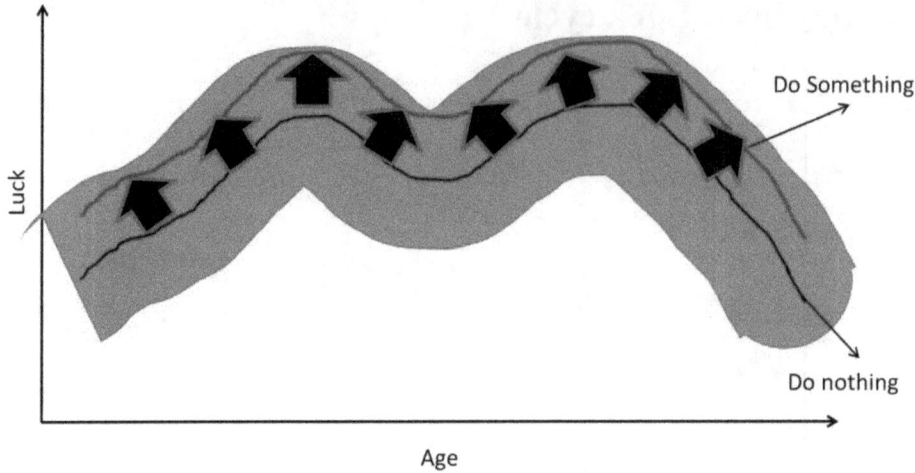

If you do nothing, then your luck will be mediocre. If you enhance it, then you push it to the maximum and get maximum return. This is regardless of whether you are in good luck or bad luck. Of course, when you are in bad luck, your returns will be less but it is better than no returns!

Bazi is diagnosis while Fengshui is prescription

Ancient Chinese Sage said: 一命, 二运, 三风水 (one: Fate, two: Luck and three: Fengshui). Basically it means you must have a good fate or destiny, if that's failed you better have good luck. However, if you have bad fate and bad luck, then your Fengshui needs to be good.

In Chinese Meta-physics, Fate and Luck can be derived from your birth date and time. This is also known as Bazi. Fengshui refers to the place that you stay or work. Although your Bazi chart is fixed, your luck is not. It is influence by the environment as well as the Yearly Energy (known as Tai Sui). Everybody knows that in life, there will always be ups and downs. There's no such thing as absolute, as in the Yin-Yang theory.

To summarized: Bazi = 一命, 二运 (one: Fate, two: Luck). Fengshui = 三风水 (three: Fengshui). As such, from Bazi, we can derive what are the ups and downs that are going to befall upon you. So Bazi can give you indications of what is going to happen. That's why Bazi is diagnosis. For example, changes in career, relationship, wealth, health etc. It could be good or it could be bad. So, if your Bazi indicates that there is windfall and if your house's Fengshui supports it, then you will get bigger windfall. On the other hand, if your house Fengshui doesn't support it, you might end up losing it. That's the prescription part of Fengshui.

However, if your house's Fengshui does not support or match your Bazi, then you will have bad "prescription". On the case of Whitney Houston, she wouldn't have died if she moves out of the house. Her house has bad "prescription" that doesn't match her Bazi. The same pattern can be found in Elizabeth Taylor's Bazi and her house.

In our Qi Men Dun Jia practice, we used Qi Men Dun Jia Bazi as basis and match it against the house's Fengshui to provide diagnosis and as well as Fengshui adjustment (proper prescription) using Qi Men Dun Jia Fengshui technique.

Qi Men Dun Jia Bazi can provide information on good location or direction for wealth. You can go to that good location to seek wealth. A good location or direction for health can help to increase your chances of getting well from illness.

In short, Qi Men Dun Jia Bazi will provide a map of your life. You have the option to adjust it by using Fengshui or through actions.

How to maximize your luck

The ancient sage had provided the formula to maximize your luck. They are:

一命，二运，三风水，四积德，五读书，六名，七相，八敬神，九交贵人，十养生.

1. Destiny
2. Luck
3. Fengshui
4. Do good deed (Karma)
5. Study
6. Good name
7. Change your look or attitudes
8. Ask for blessing (Spiritual)
9. Obtain help from networking (Nobleman)
10. Self-cultivating

Destiny and luck were covered in above. For Fengshui, it will be a wide topic. However by using Qi Men Dun Jia as a method, we can use Divination to take a sneak peep and act accordingly with you own actions. You can use Sun Tzu art of war or 36 Stratagems for strategy of action. On a macro perspective, we can use Qi Men Dun Jia Destiny Analysis and couple it with Qi Men Dun Jia Fengshui to boost your luck as well as to save guard when your luck is down. On the micro perspective, we can use Qi Men Dun Jia Date Selection to ensure you achieve the results that you want.

The ancient sage advised us to do more good deed. This is the most basic law of nature. When you do good deed like helping others, naturally when you need help, others will help you.

Study is basically to increase your knowledge. The more you learn, the better you are informed and the wiser you are. For example, if you happen to learn Qi Men Dun Jia, then you will have the knowledge to improve your life.

Cantonese has a saying: 唔怕生壞命，最怕改壞名. It means: not afraid to have poor destiny but worst is to be given a bad name. Scientifically, it has proven that your name actually influence how people perceived you. Here are two articles for further reading:

- Can your name keep you from getting hired? (http://money.cnn.com/2009/08/26/news/economy/applicant_names/)
- How names influence our destinies (http://theweek.com/article/index/225232/how-names-influence-our-destinies)

So, in Chinese Meta-Physics point of view, apart from having a name that is socially acceptable, the name has to support the person's destiny. For example, if Fire element is beneficial to a person based on destiny analysis, then the name should have fire element.

"Your attitude, not your aptitude, will determine your altitude" - Zig Ziglar. Therefore, having good attitude is important. Buddha saying: 有心无相，相由心生；有相无心，相由心灭. It means: when you have the heart but not the look, the heart will change the appearance to be better. When you have the look but not the heart, then your appearance will change to the worst. That's why your thinking and attitude will change your appearance and look. This will change people's perception about you.

Asking for blessing is basically spiritual cultivation.

The 9th is networking. Through networking, you are able to obtain help from people who are also known as your noblemen.

Last but not least, self-cultivating is the way to improve your wellbeing. This can be done by embarking in spiritual cultivation like meditation, chanting or embark in healthy life-style like Qigong practice. Healthy mind will have healthy body.

So, now you know why the same person born on the same date, time and location does not have the same destiny. This is because only the first two items (destiny and luck) are the same. The rest are different. Even twins that stay in the same house with the same parents have different karmas, names, attitudes and will meet different people as well. So many people were born on the date and time as Bill Gates but there is only one billionaire Bill Gates.

Why Destiny Reading is accurate when reading the past?

People asked me this all the time. This is because you don't have the baggage of knowing the future prior to the destiny reading. However, after a destiny reading, your subconscious mind will kicks in and without you knowing, your mind will react to the information provided during the destiny reading. In addition, you might decide to act on it instead of leaving it to destiny.

There is this book written by Yuan Liao-Fan in the 16th Century with the title: *Liao-Fan's four lessons*. This book was intended to teach his son how to recognize the true face of destiny, tell the good from the bad, correct one's faults and practice kind deeds. It also provided living proof of the rewards and outcomes of people who practiced kind deeds and cultivated virtue and humility. Basically the books told his' own experience at changing destiny. This book is translated into English and you can find it from the Internet.

How can you maximize your opportunity using Qi Men Dun Jia?

Qi Men Dun Jia Divination can provide a sneak peep of the outcome. This helps to provide information for you to take appropriate actions. Like what Sun Tzu said: *know yourself and know your enemy, you win thousand wars*. So, using every scenario as warfare, you perform Qi Men Dun Jia divination to understand your "enemy". Then you use appropriate action (know yourself) to your advantage to win the "war".

Qi Men Dun Jia Bazi can be used as basis for major decision. For example, to ensure that the house you are staying will support you in your future endeavor. You can choose a good sitting house that matches your Qi Men Dun Jia Bazi. (See Destiny Reading above).

To ensure optimum results, you can use Qi Men Dun Jia Date Selection to choose a good date and time to execute your plan. Qi Men Dun Jia Date Selection is a complex process and normally it can take weeks just to find a good date. However, I have simplified the process and created software for students to use. A good date can be found within minutes.

For precautions and lasting results, Qi Men Dun Jia Fengshui can be used. Qi Men Dun Jia bazi and Qi Men Dun Jia Fengshui can be used to enhance your bazi as well as to remedy any shortfall. For more serious problem, Qi Men Dun Jia Live Grave can be used.

Zi Ping Bazi

vs

Qi Men Dun Jia Bazi

Zi Ping Bazi

When people talks about Destiny Analysis or four pillar of destiny, everybody will think about Bazi or Zi Wei Dou Shu. The Bazi that we all know is known as Zi Ping Bazi. The current system of Destiny Analysis was based on the system enhanced by Xu Da Sheng (徐大升) or also known as Xu Zi Ping (徐子平). He lived during the Song Dynasty (960 – 1279). Before his time, people used the Year Pillar (Year Heavenly Stem and Earthly Branch) to read destiny. Xu Zi Ping rationalized and used the Day Pillar to represent the person and the rest to derived 6-relationships (Ancestors, Parents, Siblings, Children etc). He also invented the 10-gods system to provide more information. In addition, he also cleans up some of the Shen Sha system to make it more structured.

An example of Zi Ping Bazi chart is as follow:

Destiny Chart:

Hour 时	Day 日	Month 月	Year 年
丁	庚	壬	丙
丑	辰	辰	寅
辛己癸	癸戊乙	癸戊乙	戊甲丙

This was derived by using the Chinese Solar Calendar. (Note: some masters use the Lunar Calendar to plot the Destiny Chart). From the Destiny Chart, the Luck Cycle is derived:

85	75	65	55	45	35	25	15	5
癸	甲	乙	丙	丁	戊	己	庚	辛
未	申	酉	戌	亥	子	丑	寅	卯

The Luck Cycle consists of 10 years luck for each Pillar (Heavenly Stem and Earthly Branch). It gives general luck information of those 10 years. For example, from the above, Xin Mao (辛卯) is the luck from 5-14 years old.

Qi Men Dun Jia Bazi

Qi Men Dun Jia was first used by 黃帝 (the Yellow Emperor, Huáng Dì- 2697 BC to 2597 BC) around 4,500 years ago. If you refer to the introduction section, the famous people like 诸葛亮 (Zhūgě Liàng), 姜子牙 (Jiāng Zǐyá) and 張良 (Zhāng Liáng) already used Qi Men Dun Jia way before Zi Ping Bazi was invented.

A lot of people know that Qi Men Dun Jia is being used as military tools but not many people were aware that Qi Men Dun Jia can be used for destiny analysis and Fengshui as well. Why is that so? This is because in ancient time, Qi Men Dun Jia can only be used by the emperor and his advisors. Commoner who practice Qi Men Dun Jia will be executed. Hence, what I am revealing here was kept secret for nearly 4,000 years from the common Chinese and nearly 5,000 years from the Westerner or English speaking people!

Plotting a Qi Men Dun Jia chart for bazi is the same way as plotting a normal Qi Men Dun Jia chart. Just use the person birth date and time to find out the Dun and Ju. Then you it plot accordingly.

The Qi Men Dun Jia Bazi chart consists of 2 parts:

- 4 Pillars which is similar to Zi Ping Bazi
- Qi Men Dun Jia chart

4 Pillars

Hour 时	Day 日	Month 月	Year 年
丁	庚	壬	丙
丑	辰	辰	寅
辛己癸	癸戊乙	癸戊乙	戊甲丙

In Qi Men Dun Jia Bazi, the Year Heavenly Stem represents parents, Month Heavenly Stem represents siblings, Day Heavenly Stem represents yourself and Hour Heavenly Stem represents your offspring.

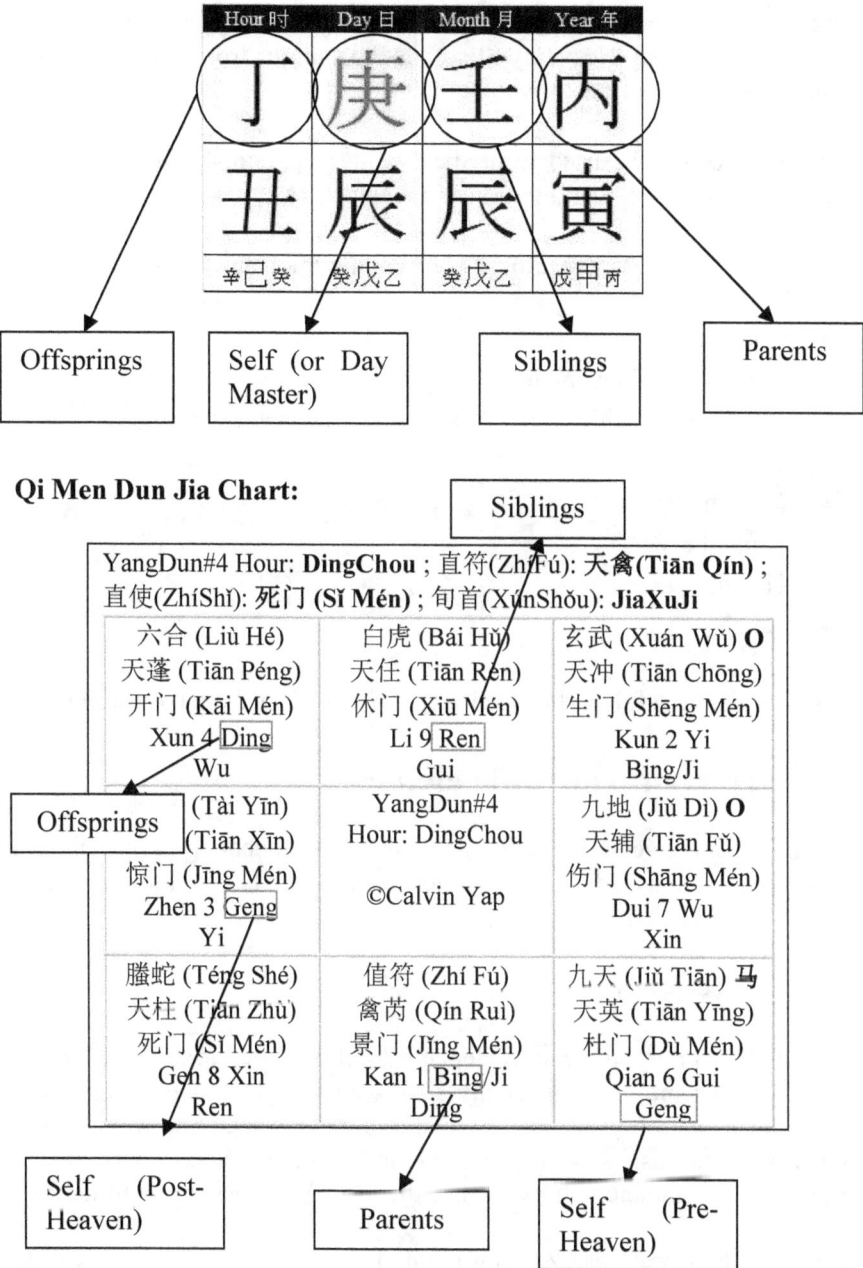

For Qi Men Dun Jia Bazi, there is no 10 years luck cycle like in Zi Ping Bazi. Your luck is derived on annual basis. As rule of thumb, as long as that particular year's Heavenly Stem and Earth Branch (also known as Tai Sui) resides in Palaces that are in restricting situation with your Day

Heavenly Stem, then we can predict that this is not a good year for you. However, if your Day Heavenly Stem has the support from annual Tai Sui, then it will be a good year for you.

The same rules can be used to predict events happening to a person. For example, changes in career, relationship, health etc.

For Qi Men Dun Jia Bazi reading, the following information can be read:

- Character
- Academic achievement
- Relationship with spouse, siblings, parents and offspring
- Career
- Wealth luck
- Annual events
- Health
- Death

The appropriate Useful God is needed for Qi Men Dun Jia bazi reading.

What are my favourable elements?

I was having a conversation with one of the new student from my Qi Men Dun Jia class, she asked me to help her derived her favourable element(s) based on her bazi chart.

I told her, "it's depends..."

She said: "What do you mean by depends? All you need to do is to look at my bazi and let me know what my strong and weak elements are. From there you can find out what are my favourable elements." She continued to plot her bazi chart using Zi Ping method via her iPhone. She showed me the 4-Pillars (or 8-Characters, hence it is called bazi) and asked me to derive.

I said: "Firstly, even I use Zi Ping method, I don't use strong or weak to read the chart. Secondly, I'm using Qi Men Dun Jia method and it's all depends on what are you looking for. A favourable element for Wealth might be different from favourable element for Health. So, what do you want?"

She was dumb folded. So, I continued to plot her Bazi chart using Qi Men Dun Jia and explained to her what her potential sickness is, where her wealth sector is and associated elements. I also advised her on her solutions to mitigate the sickness that she has. She also asked whether she has the pre-heaven luck to learn Chinese Meta-Physics. I told her yes. She ended up taking Master Ye's Bazi class instead.

YangDun#4 Hour: **DingChou** ; 直符(ZhíFú): **天禽(Tiān Qín)** ; 直使(ZhíShǐ): **死门 (Sǐ Mén)** ; 旬首(XúnShǒu): **JiaXuJi**		
六合 (Liù Hé) 天蓬 (Tiān Péng) 开门 (Kāi Mén) Xun 4 Ding Wu	白虎 (Bái Hǔ) 天任 (Tiān Rèn) 休门 (Xiū Mén) Li 9 Ren Gui	玄武 (Xuán Wǔ) **O** 天冲 (Tiān Chōng) 生门 (Shēng Mén) Kun 2 Yi Bing/Ji
太阴 (Tài Yīn) 天心 (Tiān Xīn) 惊门 (Jīng Mén) Zhen 3 Geng Yi	YangDun#4 Hour: DingChou ©Calvin Yap	九地 (Jiǔ Dì) **O** 天辅 (Tiān Fǔ) 伤门 (Shāng Mén) Dui 7 Wu Xin
螣蛇 (Téng Shé) 天柱 (Tiān Zhù) 死门 (Sǐ Mén) Gen 8 Xin Ren	值符 (Zhí Fú) 禽芮 (Qín Ruì) 景门 (Jǐng Mén) Kan 1 Bing/Ji Ding	九天 (Jiǔ Tiān) 马 天英 (Tiān Yīng) 杜门 (Dù Mén) Qian 6 Gui Geng

Using the chart above as example, her Wealth element is Earth. This is because Sheng Men is at Kun 2 Palace, which is Earth. However, Earth is also her bad element as Si Men is at Gen 8 Palace, which is Earth also. So, a Qi Men Dun Jia Bazi practitioner will have to prescribe different type of Qi Men Dun Jia Fengshui remedy based on this information.

If she wants to enhance her career, the Yong Shen (Useful God) for career is Kai Men and her Kai Men is at Xun 4 Palace.

However, the "favourable element" has to take into consideration of yearly Tai Sui etc. So, it is dynamic depending on the chart and the cycle you are in.

In Qi Men Dun Jia Fengshui we prescribe specific remedy for specific needs. There is no "favourable" or "unfavourable elements" in Qi Men Dun Jia. All are derived based on your needs at that particular point of time - coincide with the theory of Heaven, Man and Earth.

Qi Men Dun Jia Date Selection

History of Date Selection

Date Selection existed since the Xia Dynasty. It was recorded in the grand book of rites (大戴礼记). When it reached Spring and Autumn period, it became the norm for emperor to choose a date when performing major tasks. During that time, the famous emperor Gōu Jiàn had chosen a specific date to return from Wu Kingdom back to Yue Kingdom.

From Qin dynasty to Han dynasty, date selection became common. During the Eastern Han dynasty, the 6-years wooden inscribed method of 12-officers was used. They are 建 (Jiàn) – Establish, 除 (Chú) – Eliminate, 满 (Mǎn) – Full, 平 (Píng) – Balance, 定 (Dìng) – Calm, 执 (Zhí) – Initiate, 破 (Pò) – Destroy, 危 (Wēi) – Danger, 成 (Chéng) – Accomplish, 收 (Shōu) – Receive, 开 (Kāi) – Open and 闭 (Bì) – Shut. This was unearth in one of the Han dynasty's tomb.

During the Wei, Jin and North/South era where there were frequent wars and turmoils, date selection was used when deploying army.

Date Selection started to mature during the Song dynasty. In the Song dynasty calendar, the Tai Sui was officially being marked in the calendar and officially being called out as the main general for the year. In addition, warnings were given on the outcome of doing renovation on the Tai Sui sector. As such, the San Sha system was published for commoners to prevent against it.

When it reached the Qing dynasty, many types of Date Selection methods were used. All these systems produced contradict results and this confused all the people. During Kang Xi emperor's time, a famous scholar, Li Kwang Di, under the instruction of Kang Xi emperor wrote a 36- volumes of information on astrology and date selection. Later, Qian Long emperor commissioned the correction and compiled the information into 协纪辨方书 (Xié Jì Biàn Fāng Shū). The emperor also commissioned a project to publish a yearly almanac for commoners to use. Since then, date selection has been a part of day-to-day practice of all Chinese.

From the above outline of history, Qi Men Dun Jia Date Selection was never mentioned as it can only be used specifically by emperor. The method used in Qi Men Dun Jia Date Selection was recorded in 时家奇门遁甲择日术. The current system used for Date Selection by the public was different from the system used by the ancient emperor. This was because Qi Men Dun Jia system of date selection had bigger functions and the results were remarkable. All these while, this system was exclusively used by the emperor and cannot be practiced by the commoners. The reason is simple. This was because the emperor was afraid that the commoners would use it to overthrown the emperor. As such, this system was passed down by some high ranking officers that secretly transmitted the method to their descendants orally. From the history, all the major changes in dynasty were assisted by someone who practiced Qi Men Dun Jia. This is the best among the best system.

Human Aspect Action

No action, no movement, no improvement.

In a nutshell, we need to take action to have better control of our destiny. Looking at Chinese Meta-Physics and human action in a better perspective:

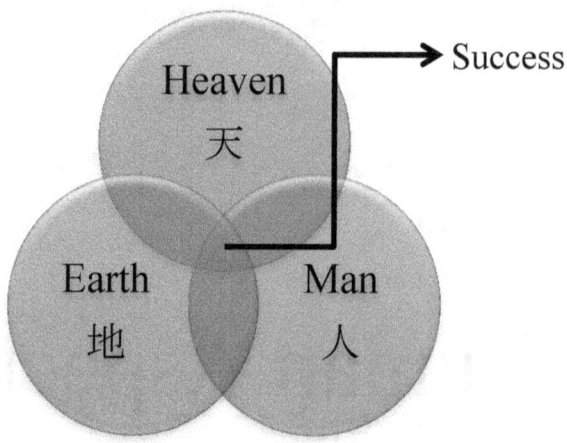

We understand that we need the support from Heaven, Earth and Man (天时、地利、人和). Mapping this support into day-to-day application, it means:

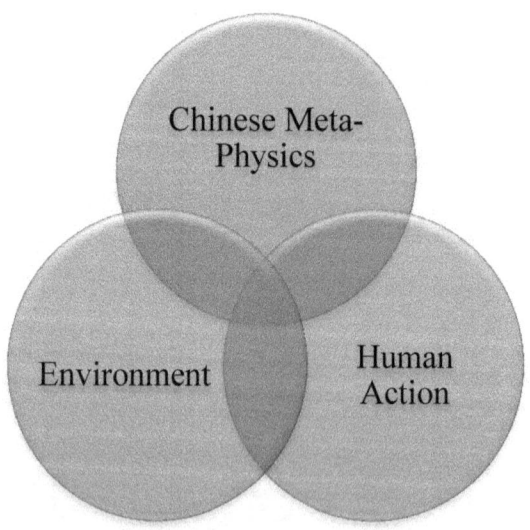

Let me explain by using a simple example. Assuming that you are Zhuge Liang and now you are in a war with your enemy. What are the tools that you will use to ensure that you will win the war? For a start, Zhuge Liang being a practitioner of Qi Men Dun Jia as well as a military strategist, you will probably make use of Qi Men Dun Jia Date Selection to choose a good date for attack. Since you are going for a war, you will probably need to understand the terrain or where the intended war is going to take place and as well as the nature of your energy. The part that describes the understanding of "Environment", in this context, is documented in the Sun Tzu Art of War (孙子兵法).

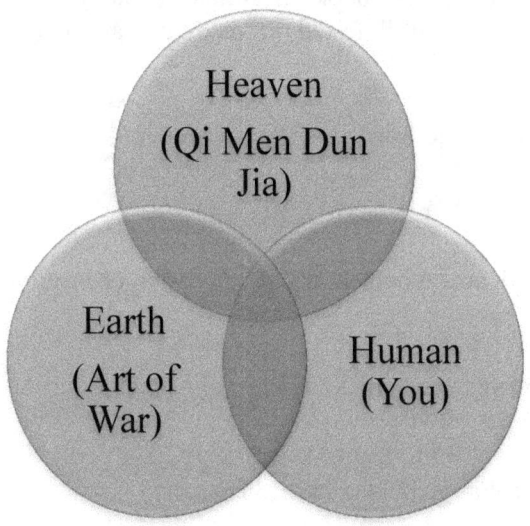

Therefore, the Art of War is the technique that can be used to understand the "Environment" or Earth aspect of the War. Then, with You (the Human Aspect) using Qi Men Dun Jia (the Heaven Aspect) together with Art of War to ensure a successful battle. As stated in the Art of War:

"天时、地利、人和，三者不得，虽胜有殃",

Which means: if there is no support from Heaven, Earth and Man, even if you win the war, there will be calamity.

In modern context, they said that business is like warfare. So, like Qi Men Dun Jia, Sun Tzu Art of War can be adopted in modern context. There are a lot of books out there that explains how Sun Tzu Art of War can be used in modern context.

Sun Tzu Art of War

Sun Tzu (544 BC – 496 BC) was a Chinese military general, strategist and philosopher who lived in the Spring and Autumn Period of ancient China. He is credited as the author of The Art of War (孙子兵法), an extremely influential ancient Chinese book on military strategy that was adopted by various generals and well tested in modern warfare (e.g. Korean war, Vietnam war etc.)

The most famous quote from Sun Tze Art of War is:

知己知彼，百戰不殆

Which means: Know yourself and know your enemy, you will win all battles.

Likewise, knowing yourself, knowing your enemy and knowing Qi Men Dun Jia, success is certain.

[7]Sun Tze Art of War is divided into 13 chapters:

Chapter	Description[8]
1	Detail Assessment and Planning (始計，始计)
2	Waging War (作戰，作战)
3	Strategic Attack (謀攻，谋攻)
4	Disposition of the Army (軍形，军形)
5	Forces (兵勢，兵势)
6	Weaknesses and Strengths (虛實，虚实)
7	Military Manoeuvres (軍爭，军争)

---

[7] From Wikipedia

[8] Using Chow-Hou

8	Variations and Adaptability (九變，九变)
9	Movement and Development of Troops (行軍，行军)
10	Terrain (地形)
11	The Nine Battlegrounds (九地)
12	Attacking with Fire (火攻)
13	Intelligence and Espionage (用間，用间)

1. **Detail Assessment and Planning** explores the five fundamental factors (the way, seasons, terrain, leadership and management) and seven elements that determine the outcome of military engagements. By thinking, assessing and comparing these points, a commander can calculate his chances of victory. Habitual deviation from these calculations will ensure failure via improper action. The text stresses that war is a very grave matter for the state and must not be commenced without due consideration.
2. **Waging War** explains how to understand the economy of warfare and how success requires winning decisive engagements quickly. This section advises that successful military campaigns require limiting the cost of competition and conflict.
3. **Strategic Attack** defines the source of strength as unity, not size, and discusses the five factors that are needed to succeed in any war. In order of importance, these critical factors are: Attack, Strategy, Alliances, Army and Cities.
4. **Disposition of the Army** explains the importance of defending existing positions until a commander is capable of advancing from those positions in safety. It teaches commanders the importance of recognizing strategic opportunities, and teaches not to create opportunities for the enemy.
5. **Forces** explain the use of creativity and timing in building an army's momentum.
6. **Weaknesses and Strengths** explain how an army's opportunities come from the openings in the environment caused by the relative weakness of the enemy and how to respond to changes in the fluid battlefield over a given area.
7. **Military Manoeuvres** explain the dangers of direct conflict and how to win those confrontations when they are forced upon the commander.

8. **Variations and Adaptability** focuses on the need for flexibility in an army's responses. It explains how to respond to shifting circumstances successfully.
9. **Movement and Development of Troops** describes the different situations in which an army finds itself as it moves through new enemy territories, and how to respond to these situations. Much of this section focuses on evaluating the intentions of others.
10. **Terrain** looks at the three general areas of resistance (distance, dangers and barriers) and the six types of ground positions that arise from them. Each of these six field positions offers certain advantages and disadvantages.
11. **The Nine Battlegrounds** describe the nine common situations (or stages) in a campaign, from scattering to deadly, and the specific focus that a commander will need in order to successfully navigate them.
12. **Attacking with Fire** explains the general use of weapons and the specific use of the environment as a weapon. This section examines the five targets for attack, the five types of environmental attack and the appropriate responses to such attacks.
13. **Intelligence and Espionage** focuses on the importance of developing good information sources, and specifies the five types of intelligence sources and how to best manage each of them

Thirty-Six Stratagems (三十六计)

Apart from Sun Tzu Art of War, the 36 stratagems can be used as the Environment or Earth component of Heaven – Man – Earth. In my day-to-day practice, I used both Sun Tzu Art of War and 36 stratagems together with Qi Men Dun Jia to achieve optimum results.

[9] The Thirty-Six Stratagems is a unique collection of ancient Chinese proverbs that describe some of the most cunning and subtle strategies ever devised. Whereas other Chinese military texts such as Sun Tzu's The Art of War focus on military organization, leadership, and battlefield tactics, the Thirty-Six Stratagems are more suitably applied in the fields of politics, diplomacy, and espionage. These proverbs describe not only battlefield

---

[9] http://www.chinastrategies.com/intro.htm

strategies, but tactics used in psychological warfare to undermine both the enemy's will to fight - and his sanity. Tactics such as the 'double cross', the 'frame job', and the 'bait and switch', can be traced back to thousands of years of Chinese history to such proverbs as 'Hide the Dagger Behind a Smile', 'Kill With a Borrowed Sword', and 'Toss out a Brick to Attract Jade' respectively. Though other Chinese military works of strategy have at least paid lip service to the Confucian notion of honour, the Thirty-Six Stratagems make no pretence of being anything but ruthless.

For the western reader the Thirty-Six Stratagems offers timeless insights into the workings of human nature under conditions of extreme stress. Many of the proverbs are based on events that occurred during China's Warring States Era (403-221 BC).

The origins of the Thirty-Six Stratagems were unknown. No author or compiler has ever been mentioned, and no date as to when it may have been written was ascertained. The first historical mention of the Thirty-Six Stratagems, dates back to the Southern Chi Dynasty (AD 489-537) where it was mentioned in the Nan Chi Shi (History of the Southern Chi Dynasty). It briefly records, "Of the 36 stratagems of Master Tan, running away is the best." Master Tan may be the famous general Tan Daoji (d. AD 436) but there is no evidence to either prove or disprove his authorship. While this was the first recorded mention of Thirty-Six Stratagems, some of the proverbs themselves are based on events that occurred up to seven hundred years earlier.

The description of Thiry-Six Strategems as adopted from Wikipedia as follow. It is being categorised into 6 chapters:

Chapter 1: Winning Stratagems (勝戰計 Shèng Zhàn Jì)

Deceive the heavens to cross the ocean (瞞天过海, Mán Tiān Guò Hǎi)

Mask your real goals, by using the ruse of a fake goal, until the real goal is achieved. Tactically, this is known as an 'open feint': in front of everyone, you point west, when your goal is actually in the east.

Besiege Wèi to rescue Zhào (围魏救赵, Wéi Wèi Jiù Zhào)

When the enemy is too strong to be attacked directly, then attack something he holds dear. Know that he cannot be superior in all things. Somewhere there is a gap in the armour, a weakness that can be attacked instead. The idea here is to avoid a head on battle with a strong enemy, and instead strike at his weakness elsewhere. This will force the strong enemy to retreat in order to support his weakness. Battling against the now tired and low-morale enemy will give a much higher chance of success.

Kill with a borrowed sword (借刀杀人, Jiè Dāo Shā Rén)

Attack using the strength of another (in a situation where using one's own strength is not favourable). Trick an ally into attacking him, bribe an official to turn traitor, or use the enemy's own strength against him. The idea here is to cause damage to the enemy by getting a 3rd party to do the deed.

Wait at leisure while the enemy labors (以逸待劳, Yǐ Yì Dài Láo)

It is an advantage to choose the time and place for battle. In this way you know when and where the battle will take place, while your enemy does not. Encourage your enemy to expend his energy in futile quests while you conserve your strength. When he is exhausted and confused, you attack with energy and purpose. The idea is to have your troops well-prepared for battle, in the same time that the enemy is rushing to fight against you. This will give your troops a huge advantage in the upcoming battle, of which you will get to select the time and place.

Loot a burning house (趁火打劫, Chèn Huǒ Dǎ Jié)

When a country is beset by internal conflicts, when disease and famine ravage the population, when corruption and crime are rampant, then it will be unable to deal with an outside threat. This is the time to attack. Keep gathering internal information about an enemy. If the enemy is currently in its weakest state ever, attack it without mercy and totally destroy it to prevent future troubles.

Make a sound in the east, then strike in the west (声东击西, Shēng Dōng Jī Xī)

In any battle the element of surprise can provide an overwhelming advantage. Even when face to face with an enemy, surprise can still be employed by attacking where he least expects it. To do this you must create an expectation in the enemy's mind through the use of a feint. The idea here is to get the enemy to focus his forces in a location, and then attack elsewhere which would be weakly defended.

Chapter 2: Enemy Dealing Stratagems (敵戰計)

Create something from nothing (无中生有, Wú Zhōng Shēng Yǒu)

A plain lie. Make somebody believe there was something when there is in fact nothing. One method of using this strategy is to create an illusion of something's existence, while it does not exist. Another method is to create an illusion that something does not exist, while it does.

Openly repair the gallery roads, but sneak through the passage of Chencang (明修栈道,暗渡陈仓, Míng Xiū Zhàn Dào, An Dù Chén Cāng)

Deceive the enemy with an obvious approach that will take a very long time, while surprising him by taking a shortcut and sneak up to him. As the enemy concentrates on the decoy, he will miss you sneaking up to him. This tactic is an extension of the "Make a sound in the east, then strike in the west" tactic. But instead of simply spreading misinformation to draw the enemy's attention, physical baits are used to increase the enemy's certainty on the misinformation. These baits must be easily seen by the enemy, to ensure that they draw the enemy's attention. At the same time, the baits must act as if they are meant to do what they were falsely doing, to avoid drawing the enemy's suspicion.

Watch the fires burning across the river (隔岸观火, Gé An Guān Huǒ)

Delay entering the field of battle until all the other players has become exhausted fighting amongst them. Then go in at full strength and pick up the pieces.

Hide a knife behind a smile (笑里藏刀, Xlào Lǐ Cáng Dāo)

Charm and ingratiate yourself to your enemy. When you have gained his trust, move against him in secret.

Sacrifice the plum tree to preserve the peach tree (李代桃僵, Lǐ Dài Táo Jiāng)

There are circumstances in which you must sacrifice short-term objectives in order to gain the long-term goal. This is the scapegoat strategy whereby someone else suffers the consequences so that the rest do not.

Take the opportunity to pilfer a goat (顺手牵羊, Shùn Shǒu Qiān Yáng)

While carrying out your plans be flexible enough to take advantage of any opportunity that presents itself, however small, and avail yourself of any profit, however slight.

Chapter 3: Attacking Stratagems (攻戰計)

Stomp the grass to scare the snake (打草惊蛇, Dá Cǎo Jīng Shé)

Do something unaimed, but spectacular ("hitting the grass") to provoke a response of the enemy ("startle the snake"), thereby giving away his plans or position, or just taunt him. Do something unusual, strange, and unexpected as this will arouse the enemy's suspicion and disrupt his thinking. More widely used as "[Do not] startle the snake by hitting the grass". An imprudent act will give your position or intentions away to the enemy.

Borrow a corpse to resurrect the soul (借尸还魂, Jiè Shī Huán Hún)

Take an institution, a technology, a method, or even an ideology that has been forgotten or discarded and appropriate it for your own purpose. Revive something from the past by giving it a new purpose or bring to life old ideas, customs, or traditions and reinterpret them to fit your purposes.

Entice the tiger to leave its mountain lair (调虎离山, Diào Hǔ Lí Shān)

Never directly attack an opponent whose advantage is derived from its position. Instead lure him away from his position thus separating him from his source of strength.

In order to capture, one must let loose (欲擒故纵, Yù Qín Gū Zòng)

Cornered prey will often mount a final desperate attack. To prevent this you let the enemy believe he still has a chance for freedom. His will to fight is thus dampened by his desire to escape. When in the end the freedom is proven a falsehood the enemy's morale will be defeated and he will surrender without a fight.

Tossing out a brick to get a jade gem (抛砖引玉, Pāo Zhuān Yǐn Yù)

Bait someone by making him believe he gains something or just make him react to it ("toss out a brick") and obtain something valuable from him in return ("get a jade gem").

Defeat the enemy by capturing their chief (擒贼擒王, Qín Zéi Qín Wáng)

If the enemy's army is strong but is allied to the commander only by money, superstition or threats, then take aim at the leader. If the commander falls the rest of the army will disperse or come over to your side. If, however, they are allied to the leader through loyalty then beware, the army can continue to fight on after his death out of vengeance.

Chapter 4: Chaos Stratagems (混戰計)

Remove the firewood from under the pot (釜底抽薪, Fǔ Dǐ Chōu Xīn)

Take out the leading argument or asset of someone; "steal someone's thunder". This is the very essence of indirect approach: instead of attacking enemy's fighting forces, the attacks are directed against his ability to wage war.

Disturb the water and catch a fish (混水摸鱼, Hún Shuǐ Mō Yú)

Create confusion and use this confusion to further your own goals.

Slough off the cicada's golden shell (金蝉脱壳, Jīn Chán Tuō Qiào)

Mask yourself. Either leave one's distinctive traits behind, thus becoming inconspicuous, or masquerade as something or someone else. This strategy is mainly used to escape from enemy of superior strength.

Shut the door to catch the thief (关门捉贼, Guān Mén Zhuō Zéi)

To capture your enemy, or more generally in fighting wars, to deliver the final blow to your enemy, you must plan prudently if you want to succeed. Do not rush into action. Before you "move in for the kill", first cut off your enemy's escape routes, and cut off any routes through which outside help can reach them.

Befriend a distant state while attacking a neighbour (远交近攻, Yuǎn Jiāo Jìn Gōng)

It is known that nations that border each other become enemies while nations separated by distance and obstacles make better allies. When you are the strongest in one field, your greatest threat is from the second strongest in your field, not the strongest from another field.

Obtain safe passage to conquer the State of Guo (假道伐虢, Jiǎ Dào Fá Guó)

Borrow the resources of an ally to attack a common enemy. Once the enemy is defeated, use those resources to turn on the ally that lent you them in the first place.

Chapter 5: Proximate Stratagems (並戰計)

Replace the beams with rotten timbers (偷梁换柱, Tōu Liáng Huàn Zhù)

Disrupt the enemy's formations, interfere with their methods of operations, change the rules in which they are used to follow, go contrary to their standard training. In this way you remove the supporting pillar, the common link that makes a group of men an effective fighting force.

Point at the mulberry tree while cursing the locust tree (指桑骂槐, Zhǐ Sāng Mà Huái)

To discipline, control, or warn others whose status or position excludes them from direct confrontation; use analogy and innuendo. Without directly naming names, those accused cannot retaliate without revealing their complicity.

Feign madness but keep your balance (假痴不癲, Jiǎ Chī Bù Diān)

Hide behind the mask of a fool, a drunk, or a madman to create confusion about your intentions and motivations. Lure your opponent into underestimating your ability until, overconfident, he drops his guard. Then you may attack.

Remove the ladder when the enemy has ascended to the roof (上屋抽梯, Shàng Wū Chōu Tī)

With baits and deceptions, lure your enemy into treacherous terrain. Then cut off his lines of communication and avenue of escape. To save himself, he must fight both your own forces and the elements of nature.

Deck the tree with false blossoms (树上开花, Shù Shàng Kāi Huā)

Tying silk blossoms on a dead tree gives the illusion that the tree is healthy. Through the use of artifice and disguise, make something of no value appear valuable; of no threat appear dangerous; of no use appear useful.

Make the host and the guest exchange roles (反客为主, Fǎn Kè Wéi Zhǔ)

Usurp leadership in a situation where you are normally subordinate. Infiltrate your target. Initially, pretend to be a guest to be accepted, but develop from inside and become the owner later.

Chapter 6: Desperate Stratagems (敗戰計)

The beauty trap (Honeypot)[(美人计, Měi Rén Jì)

Send your enemy beautiful women to cause discord within his camp. This strategy can work on three levels. First, the ruler becomes so enamoured with the beauty that he neglects his duties and allows his vigilance to wane. Second, other males at court will begin to display aggressive behaviour that inflames minor differences hindering co-operation and destroying morale. Third, other females at court, motivated by jealousy and envy, begin to plot intrigues further exacerbating the situation.

The empty fort strategy (空城计, Kōng Chéng Jì)

When the enemy is superior in numbers and your situation is such that you expect to be overrun at any moment, then drop all pretense of military preparedness, act calmly and taunt the enemy, so that the enemy will think you have a huge ambush hidden for them. It works best by acting calm and at ease when your enemy expects you to be tense. This ploy is only successful if in most cases you do have a powerful hidden force and only sparsely use the empty fort strategy.

Let the enemy's own spy sow discord in the enemy camp (反间计, Fǎn Jiàn Jì)

Undermine your enemy's ability to fight by secretly causing discord between him and his friends, allies, advisors, family, commanders, soldiers, and population. While he is preoccupied settling internal disputes, his ability to attack or defend, is compromised.

Inflict injury on oneself to win the enemy's trust (苦肉计, Kǔ Ròu Jì)

Pretending to be injured has two possible applications. In the first, the enemy is lulled into relaxing his guard since he no longer considers you to be an immediate threat. The second is a way of ingratiating yourself to your enemy by pretending the injury was caused by a mutual enemy.

Chain stratagems (连环计, Lián Huán Jì)

In important matters, one should use several stratagems applied simultaneously after another as in a chain of stratagems. Keep different plans operating in an overall scheme; however, in this manner if any one strategy fails, then the chain breaks and the whole scheme fails.

If all else fails, retreat (走为上, Zǒu Wéi Shàng)

If it becomes obvious that your current course of action will lead to defeat, then retreat and regroup. When your side is losing, there are only three choices remaining: surrender, compromise, or escape. Surrender is complete defeat, compromise is half defeat, but escape is not defeat. As long as you are not defeated, you still have a chance. This is the most famous of the stratagems, immortalized in the form of a Chinese idiom: "Of the Thirty-Six Stratagems, fleeing is best" (三十六计，走为上计).

Qi Men Dun Jia Case Studies

Divination Cases

Case 1: House Audit

Background

I was invited to a friend house and during our casual discussion, he asked me what I thought about his house Fengshui. I plotted a Qi Men Dun Jia chart based on the time he asked this question. The house is facing North, sitting South.
The date and time when question asked was on: 23rd May 2010 at 12:26

The chart is as follow:

Hour	Day	Month	Year
Wu	Gui	Xin	Geng
Wu	You	Si	Yin

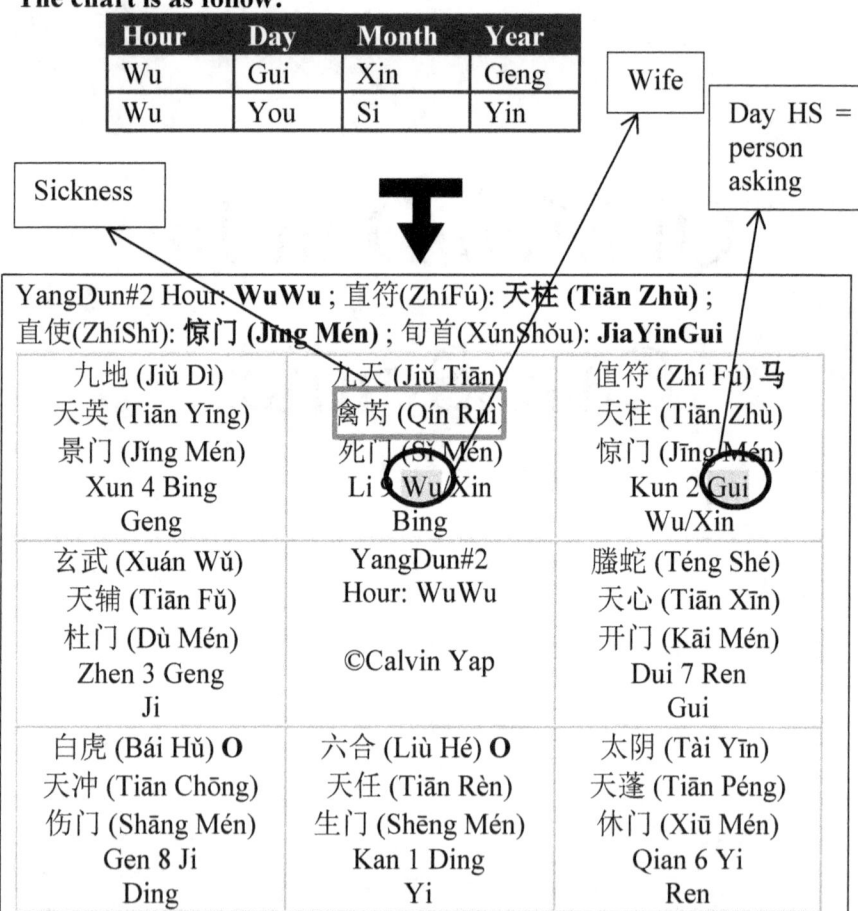

Analysis

The person asking is represented by the Day Heavenly Stem, Gui. In this case, it is at Kun 2 Palace. The house is facing North, sitting South. At the South Palace Li 9, there is Wu, which represents his wife. (The spouse of Gui is Wu because Wu combines with Gui).

At Li 9 Palace, there are 天芮 (Tiān Ruì) and 九天 (Jiǔ Tiān). 天芮 (Tiān Ruì) represents sickness star and Li 9 Palace represents the head. Therefore, I deduced that his wife had frequent headache. In addition, the headache was quite severe as 天芮 (Tiān Ruì) with 九天 (Jiǔ Tiān) means sickness was expanded.

He later told me that his wife had constant migraine and relied a lot on medication to control. Her migraine was quite serious.

A set of Fengshui remedy based on Qi Men Dun Jia was provided.

Case 2: House Audit – Child always fall sick

Background

My daughter's tuition teacher approached me for a house audit. She said her son tends to fall sick frequently. Every time he recovered, he would fall sick again in a few days' time. In addition, she noticed that her son talked to himself.

The date and time when question asked was on: 26th March 2013 at 21:00

The chart is as follow:

Hour	Day	Month	Year
Ji	Xin	Yi	Gui
Hai	Mao	Mao	Si

YangDun#6 Hour: **JiHai** ; 直符(ZhíFú): **天英 (Tiān Yīng)** ; 直使(ZhíShǐ): **景门 (Jǐng Mén)** ; 旬首(XúnShǒu): **JiaWuXin**

玄武 (Xuán Wǔ) O 马 天任 (Tiān Rèn) 伤门 (Shāng Mén) Xun 4 Geng Bing	九地 (Jiǔ Dì) 天冲 (Tiān Chōng) 杜门 (Dù Mén) Li 9 Ding Xin	九天 (Jiǔ Tiān) 天辅 (Tiān Fǔ) 景门 (Jǐng Mén) Kun 2 Bing Gui/Yi
白虎 (Bái Hǔ) 天蓬 (Tiān Péng) 生门 (Shēng Mén) Zhen 3 Ren Ding	YangDun#6 Hour: JiHai ©Calvin Yap	值符 (Zhí Fú) 天英 (Tiān Yīng) 死门 (Sǐ Mén) Dui 7 Xin Ji
六合 (Liù Hé) 天心 (Tiān Xīn) 休门 (Xiū Mén) Gen 8 Wu Geng	太阴 (Tài Yīn) 天柱 (Tiān Zhù) 开门 (Kāi Mén) Kan 1 Ji Ren	螣蛇 (Téng Shé) 禽芮 (Qín Ruì) 惊门 (Jīng Mén) Qian 6 Gui/Yi Wu

Spirit

Hour HS = son

Analysis

She was asking about her son, so we looked at the Hour Heavenly Stem. Hour Heavenly Stem is Ji which is at Kan 1 Palace. In that palace there is 太阴 (Tài Yīn) and 太阴 (Tài Yīn) represents spirit or ghost. So, I told her that her son might have close encounter with supernatural that caused his frequent sickness. I advised her to bring her son to her religious of choice for help. She brought her son to a Buddhist temple for regular blessing. 2 weeks later, she told me her son was much better and didn't talk to himself anymore.

Her son bazi chart as follow:

Hour	Day	Month	Year
Ren	Ji	Bing	Geng
Shen	You	Xu	Yin

Tai Yin with Day Master; might have ability to see spirit

Day HS = son

YinDun#5 Hour: **RenShen** ; 直符(ZhíFú): **天禽(Tiān Qín)** ;
直使(ZhíShǐ): **死门 (Sǐ Mén)** ; 旬首(XúnShǒu): **JiaZiWu**

玄武 (Xuán Wǔ) 天蓬 (Tiān Péng) 生门 (Shēng Mén) Xun 4 Ren Ji	白虎 (Bái Hǔ) 天任 (Tiān Rèn) 伤门 (Shāng Mén) Li 9 Ding Gui	六合 (Liù Hé) 天冲 (Tiān Chōng) 杜门 (Dù Mén) Kun 2 Geng Xin/Wu
九地 (Jiǔ Dì) 天心 (Tiān Xīn) 休门 (Xiū Mén) Zhen 3 Yi Geng	YinDun#5 Hour: RenShen ©Calvin Yap	太阴 (Tài Yīn) 天辅 (Tiān Fǔ) 景门 (Jǐng Mén) Dui 7 Ji Bing
九天 (Jiǔ Tiān) 马 天柱 (Tiān Zhù) 开门 (Kāi Mén) Gen 8 Bing Ding	值符 (Zhí Fú) 禽芮 (Qín Ruì) 惊门 (Jīng Mén) Kan 1 Xln/Wu Ren	螣蛇 (Téng Shé) O 天英 (Tiān Yīng) 死门 (Sǐ Mén) Qian 6 Gui Yi

Her son Day Master is Ji which is at Dui 7 Palace. In the palace, there is 太阴 (Tài Yīn). This would mean that her son might have the ability to "see" spirit or ghost.

Case 3: Bus breakdown

Background

I was waiting for my condo bus, I've been waiting longer than usual and the bus still hasn't arrived. I received a text message from my wife and was informed that the bus had broken down. I have 2 choices; I either walk to the train station which was about 2km away or wait for replacement bus.

I decided to do a divination to see if the replacement bus would be coming.

The date and time when question asked was on: 8th April 2010 at 07:00

The chart is as follow:

Hour	Day	Month	Year
Bing	Wu	Geng	Geng
Chen	Zi	Chen	Yin

Bus and not in Kong or Horse

YangDun#1 Hour: **BingChen** ; 直符(ZhíFú): **天心 (Tiān Xīn)** ; 直使(ZhíShǐ): **开门 (Kāi Mén)** ; 旬首(XúnShǒu): **JiaYinGui**

太阴 (Tài Yīn) 天任 (Tiān Rèn) 生门 (Shēng Mén) Xun 4 Bing Xin	六合 (Liù Hé) 天冲 (Tiān Chōng) 伤门 (Shāng Mén) Li 9 Geng Yi	白虎 (Bái Hǔ) 天辅 (Tiān Fǔ) 杜门 (Dù Mén) Kun 2 Xin Ji/Ren
螣蛇 (Téng Shé) 天蓬 (Tiān Péng) 休门 (Xiū Mén) Zhen 3 Wu Geng	YangDun#1 Hour: BingChen ©Calvin Yap	玄武 (Xuán Wǔ) 天英 (Tiān Yīng) 景门 (Jǐng Mén) Dui 7 Yi Ding
值符 (Zhí Fú) O 马 天心 (Tiān Xīn) 开门 (Kāi Mén) Gen 8 Gui Bing	九天 (Jiǔ Tiān) O 天柱 (Tiān Zhù) 惊门 (Jīng Mén) Kan 1 Ding Wu	九地 (Jiǔ Dì) 禽芮 (Qín Ruì) 死门 (Sǐ Mén) Qian 6 Ji/Ren Gui

Analysis

The Yong Shen (Useful God) for Bus is 伤门 (Shāng Mén), which is at Li 9 Palace. In that palace there is Geng, it represents problem. Hence, the bus broke down because of arising problem.

However, there is no Kong or Horse in that palace. Therefore, I deduced that the replacement bus should be coming.

After 10 minutes of waiting, the replacement bus came and I boarded the bus and managed to reach office on time. If I had not done a divination, I would have walk to the train station. It would take me 20 minutes and ended up with a sweaty shirt!

Case 4: Male or Female doctor

Background

I was waiting for my turn to see a doctor at the clinic. There were 2 doctors; 1 male and 1 female. Out of curiosity, I plotted a Qi Men Dun Jia chart to see which doctor I could be seeing.

The date and time when question asked was on: 5th April 2010 at 10:00

The chart is as follow:

Hour	Day	Month	Year
Xin	Yi	Geng	Geng
Si	You	Chen	Yin

Doctor

Kun2 = Female

YangDun#1 Hour: **XinSi** ; 直符(ZhíFú): **天芮 (Tiān Ruì)** ;
直使(ZhíShǐ): **死门 (Sǐ Mén)** ; 旬首(XúnShǒu): **JiaXuJi**

值符 (Zhí Fú) 禽芮 (Qín Ruì) 景门 (Jǐng Mén) Xun 4 Ji/Ren Xin	腾蛇 (Téng Shé) 天柱 (Tiān Zhù) 死门 (Sǐ Mén) Li 9 Ding Yi	太阴 (Tài Yīn) O 天心 (Tiān Xīn) 惊门 (Jīng Mén) Kun 2 Gui Ji/Ren
九天 (Jiǔ Tiān) 天英 (Tiān Yīng) 杜门 (Dù Mén) Zhen 3 Yi Geng	YangDun#1 Hour: XinSi ©Calvin Yap	六合 (Liù Hé) O 天蓬 (Tiān Péng) 开门 (Kāi Mén) Dui 7 Wu Ding
九地 (Jiǔ Dì) 天辅 (Tiān Fǔ) 伤门 (Shāng Mén) Gen 8 Xin Bing	玄武 (Xuán Wǔ) 天冲 (Tiān Chōng) 生门 (Shēng Mén) Kan 1 Geng Wu	白虎 (Bái Hǔ) 马 天任 (Tiān Rèn) 休门 (Xiū Mén) Qian 6 Bing Gui

Analysis

The Yong Shen or Useful God for doctor is 天心 (Tiān Xīn). In this case, it is at Kun 2 Palace. Kun 2 Palace represents female. So, I deduced that the doctor that I would be seeing is female.

I ended up seeing the female doctor.

Case 5: Tour bus stuck at Yang Ming Shan, Taipei

Background

I was in Taipei for vacation and was at Yang Ming Shan when the tour bus was trying to perform a 3-point turn failed and was stuck in a narrow road. The tour guide called for help and a crane was supposed to lift the bus out of the situation. The rest of the tour members were reckless and worried as we were stuck at some remote location. So, I plotted a Qi Men Dun Jia chart to see when we would get out of the situation.

The date and time when question asked was on: 19th April 2014 at 16:00

The chart is as follow:

Hour	Day	Month	Year
Jia	Geng	Wu	Jia
Shen	Shen	Chen	Wu

4:40pm is at Li 9 Palace

YangDun#7 Hour: **JiaShen** ; 直符(ZhíFú): 天英 **(Tiān Yīng)** ;
值使(ZhíShǐ): 景门 **(Jǐng Mén)** ; 旬首(XúnShǒu): **JiaShenGeng**

九天 (Jiǔ Tiān) 天辅 (Tiān Fǔ) 杜门 (Dù Mén) Xun 4 Ding Ding	值符 (Zhí Fú) O 天英 (Tiān Yīng) 景门 (Jǐng Mén) Li 9 Geng Geng	螣蛇 (Téng Shé) O 禽芮 (Qín Ruì) 死门 (Sǐ Mén) Kun 2 Ren/Bing Ren/Bing
九地 (Jiǔ Dì) 天冲 (Tiān Chōng) 伤门 (Shāng Mén) Zhen 3 Gui Gui	YangDun#7 Hour: JiaShen **Fu Yin** ©Calvin Yap	太阴 (Tài Yīn) 天柱 (Tiān Zhù) 惊门 (Jīng Mén) Dui 7 Wu Wu
玄武 (Xuán Wǔ) 马 天任 (Tiān Rèn) 生门 (Shēng Mén) Gen 8 Ji Ji	白虎 (Bái Hǔ) 天蓬 (Tiān Péng) 休门 (Xiū Mén) Kan 1 Xin Xin	六合 (Liù Hé) 天心 (Tiān Xīn) 开门 (Kāi Mén) Qian 6 Yi Yi

- Si = 4:30 pm
- Chen = 4:20 pm
- Mao = 4:10 pm
- Yin = 4:00 pm
- Chou = 3:50 pm
- Zi = 3:40 pm
- Hai = 3:30 pm
- Xu = 3:20 pm
- You = Dui 7 = 3:10pm
- Shen = Kun 2 = 3pm

Analysis

I got a Fu Yin chart. Fu Yin chart means it's stagnant, stuck and/or suffering. Getting stuck at a remote location was definitely a suffering. In addition, the bus was stuck, so it matched the Fu Yin chart.

Based on the chart above, I predicted that the crane should come and lift the bus out by 4:50pm.

From the chart, the Day and Hour Heavenly Stem are at Li 9 Palace and in Kong. With a Fu Yin chart and in Kong, it means that help won't be coming soon.

For calculation of time, we used the simplify method of one Earthly Branch = 10 minutes. The hour is Jia Shen hour (3pm to 4:59pm). So, Shen hour starts at 3pm and Shen is at Kun 2 Palace. With calculation of 10 minutes for each EB, by 4:40pm, it will be at Li 9 Palace. This will then fill up the Kong. As such, I deduced that help should arrive between 4:40pm – 4:50pm.

We left the place at 4:47pm and the whole bus was amazed by the power of Qi Men Dun Jia.

Case 6: Sickness Diagnostic

Background

I made an appointment to meet up with my student for breakfast as I wanted to pass her something. She sent a text message saying that she can't make it because she needed to bring her mother to the hospital. She said her mother was in pain and she didn't know what was wrong. I plotted a Qi Men Dun Jia chart and I told her that something might be stuck at her stomach area and insisted that the doctor perform a scan on that area. It was better to be safe then sorry.

The date and time when question asked was on: 12th uly 2013 at 08:12

The chart is as follow:

Hour	Day	Month	Year
Wu	Ji	Ji	Gui
Chen	Mao	Wei	Si

Sickness with Du Men at Kun 2 Palace. Kun 2 = Stomach. Something is stuck in the Stomach.

YinDun#8 Hour: **WuChen** ; 直符(ZhíFú): 天任 **(Tiān Rèn)** ;
直使(ZhíShǐ): 生门 **(Shēng Mén)** ; 旬首(XúnShǒu): **JiaZiWu**

九地 (Jiǔ Dì) 天辅 (Tiān Fǔ) 生门 (Shēng Mén) Xun 4 Ren Ren	玄武 (Xuán Wǔ) 天英 (Tiān Yīng) 伤门 (Shāng Mén) Li 9 Yi Yi	白虎 (Bái Hǔ) 禽芮 (Qín Ruì) 杜门 (Dù Mén) Kun 2 Ding/Xin Ding/Xin
九天 (Jiǔ Tiān) 天冲 (Tiān Chōng) 休门 (Xiū Mén) Zhen 3 Gui Gui	YinDun#8 Hour: WuChen **Fu Yin** ©Calvin Yap	六合 (Liù Hé) 天柱 (Tiān Zhù) 景门 (Jǐng Mén) Dui 7 Ji Ji
值符 (Zhí Fú) 马 天任 (Tiān Rèn) 开门 (Kāi Mén) Gen 8 Wu Wu	螣蛇 (Téng Shé) 天蓬 (Tiān Péng) 惊门 (Jīng Mén) Kan 1 Bing Bing	太阴 (Tài Yīn) O 天心 (Tiān Xīn) 死门 (Sǐ Mén) Qian 6 Geng Geng

Tian Xin = Doctor. In Kong, with Si Men and Tai Yin

Analysis

This is a Fu Yin chart. It means, stuck and suffering. So, her mother was suffering in pain.

The Yong Shen (Useful God) for sickness is 天芮 (Tiān Ruì) and it is at Kun 2 Palace with 白虎 (Bái Hǔ) and 杜门 (Dù Mén). In addition, there is Xin. Kun 2 Palace means stomach area. 杜门 (Dù Mén) means stuck. Xin also means growth. Therefore, I deduced that there might be growth which could be stuck at the stomach area.

The Yong Shen (Useful God) for doctor is 天心 (Tiān Xīn) which is at Qian 6 Palace is with 死门 (Sǐ Mén), 太阴 (Tài Yīn) and in Kong. 死门 (Sǐ Mén) means stubborn, so the doctor might not want to listen. 太阴 (Tài Yīn) and Kong also means the doctor didn't bother to check further. In the text message to her, I told her to insist the doctor to perform a scan mainly because from the chart, I deduced that the doctor might not want to perform a scan.

Weeks later, I received an email from my student saying that it was confirmed that after the scan it was a polyp or soft stone near the gall bladder. Initially, the doctor was reluctant to perform the scan and was only interested in treating her mother's right arm pain since that is his speciality. He only performed the scan after my student insistence.

Case 7: Colleague giving birth timing

Background

On 5th June 2012, Tuesday at around 3pm, I noticed that my pregnant colleague was not in office. So, I decided to check on her by sending her a text message. I asked her when was she due for delivery. She said, the gynecologist told her that it is most probably end of the week.

I decided to plot a Qi Men Dun Jia chart and based on the chart, I told her that she might be admitted to hospital between 5-7pm and the baby would be born the next day between 11-1pm.

The date and time when question asked was on: 5th June 2012 at 15:00

The chart is as follow:

Hour	Day	Month	Year
Wu	Ding	Bing	Ren
Shen	You	Wu	Chen

Sheng Men is the Yong Shen for gives birth with Tian Xin, the Yong Shen for doctor.

YangDun#6 Hour: **WuShen** ; 直符(ZhíFú): **天蓬 (Tiān Péng)** ; 直使(ZhíShǐ): **休门 (Xiū Mén)** ; 旬首(XúnShǒu): **JiaChenRen**

白虎 (Bái Hǔ) 天英 (Tiān Yīng) 惊门 (Jǐng Mén) Xun 4 Xin Bing	玄武 (Xuán Wǔ) 禽芮 (Qín Ruì) 开门 (Kāi Mén) Li 9 Gui/Yi Xin	九地 (Jiǔ Dì) 天柱 (Tiān Zhù) 休门 (Xiū Mén) Kun 2 Ji Gui/Yi
六合 (Liù Hé) O 天辅 (Tiān Fǔ) 死门 (Sǐ Mén) Zhen 3 Bing Ding	YangDun#6 Hour: WuShen ©Calvin Yap	九天 (Jiǔ Tiān) 天心 (Tiān Xīn) 生门 (Shēng Mén) Dui 7 Wu Ji
太阴 (Tài Yīn) O 马 天冲 (Tiān Chōng) 景门 (Jǐng Mén) Gen 8 Ding Geng	螣蛇 (Téng Shé) 天任 (Tiān Rèn) 杜门 (Dù Mén) Kan 1 Geng Ren	值符 (Zhí Fú) 天蓬 (Tiān Péng) 伤门 (Shāng Mén) Qian 6 Ren Wu

Analysis

The matter asked was giving birth. Based on the chart, the Hour Heavenly Stem is Wu which is at Dui 7 Palace with 生门 (Shēng Mén), 九天 (Jiǔ Tiān) and 天心 (Tiān Xīn). 生门 (Shēng Mén) is also the Yong Shen (Useful God) for giving birth. 天心 (Tiān Xīn) is the Yong Shen (Useful God) for doctor. So, the matter asked was giving birth, so based on the hour Heavenly Stem palace, it showed that she will be giving birth soon.

Dui 7 Palace is where You Earthly Branch is. You Earthly Branch is between 5-7pm. As such, I predicted that she might go into labour at You hour.

Why her son will be born the next day at Wu Hour? The chart for next day Wu hour as follow:

Hour	Day	Month	Year
Wu	Wu	Bing	Ren
Wu	Xu	Wu	Chen

From the plotted chart, Wu Heavenly Stem is at Dui 7 Palace with 生门 (Shēng Mén), so the baby should be born in the Wu Heavenly Stem Day or Hour. The next day is Wu Xu day and Wu Wu hour. Therefore, I predicted that her son would be born the next day, Wu hour.

At first she didn't believe me and she brushed it aside. At 6pm, I received a text message from her saying that her water bag was leaking and she is in hospital. Her son was born the next day at 11:17 am.

Case 8: Colleague worrying about her health

Background

During a casual chat after lunch, one of my colleagues was worried about her health. So, I plotted a Qi Men Dun Jia chart. I told her that she was having problem with her respiratory track and most likely required surgery. She said she had an operation recently. I told her that she should be fine and there's nothing she should worry about.

The date and time when question asked was on: 5th Feb 2010 at 14:00

The chart is as follow:

Hour	Day	Month	Year
Yi	Bing	Wu	Geng
Wei	Xu	Yin	Yin

YangDun#5 Hour: **YiWei** ; 直符(ZhíFú): 天任 (**Tiān Rèn**) ;
直使(ZhíShǐ): 生门 (**Shēng Mén**) ; 旬首(XúnShǒu): **JiaWuXin**

值符 (Zhí Fú) O 马 天任 (Tiān Rèn) 休门 (Xiū Mén) Xun 4 Xin Yi	螣蛇 (Téng Shé) 天冲 (Tiān Chōng) 生门 (Shēng Mén) Li 9 Bing Ren	太阴 (Tài Yīn) 天辅 (Tiān Fǔ) 伤门 (Shāng Mén) Kun 2 Yi Ding/Wu
九天 (Jiǔ Tiān) 天蓬 (Tiān Péng) 开门 (Kāi Mén) Zhen 3 Gui Bing	YangDun#5 Hour: YiWei ©Calvin Yap	六合 (Liù Hé) 天英 (Tiān Yīng) 杜门 (Dù Mén) Dui 7 Ren Geng
九地 (Jiǔ Dì) 天心 (Tiān Xīn) 惊门 (Jīng Mén) Gen 8 Ji Xin	玄武 (Xuán Wǔ) 天柱 (Tiān Zhù) 死门 (Sǐ Mén) Kan 1 Geng Gui	白虎 (Bái Hǔ) 禽芮 (Qín Ruì) 景门 (Jǐng Mén) Qian 6 Ding/Wu Ji

Tian Rui represents Sickness, with Jing Men means there is blood calamity.

Analysis

The Yong Shen (Useful God) for sickness is 天芮 (Tiān Ruì) which is at Qian 6 Palace with 白虎 (Bái Hǔ) and 景门 (Jǐng Mén). Qian 6 Palace also means respiratory track. Therefore, I predicted that she had respiratory problem. Her sickness was quite serious as there is 白虎 (Bái Hǔ). In addition, there is 景门 (Jǐng Mén), which represents blood related calamity. Hence, her sickness required surgery.

I deduced that she would be fine as the Day Heavenly Stem which represents her is Bing and is at Li 9 Palace with 生门 (Shēng Mén). In addition, Li 9 Palace is restricting Qian 6 Palace (Fire restrict Metal). Therefore, her sickness should be under control.

Case 9: Haunted house

Background

A friend came over for visiting and during casual discussion about her new place, she asked about her house Fengshui. I plotted a Qi Men Dun Jia chart and told her that her house Fengshui had problem. She told me that her daughter was afraid of going into a room which was in the east sector of the house. I told her that her house was potentially haunted.

The date and time when question asked was on: 6th July 2010 at 22:00

The Chart is as follow:

Hour	Day	Month	Year
Xin	Ding	Ren	Geng
Hai	Si	Wu	Yin

Day HS with Tai Yin, this place has spirit

YinDun#3 Hour: **XinHai** ; 直符(ZhíFú): **天任 (Tiān Rèn)** ;
直使(ZhíShǐ): **生门 (Shēng Mén)** ; 旬首(XúnShǒu): **JiaChenRen**

螣蛇 (Téng Shé) 马 天蓬 (Tiān Péng) 景门 (Jǐng Mén) Xun 4 Geng Yi	值符 (Zhí Fú) 天任 (Tiān Rèn) 死门 (Sǐ Mén) Li 9 Ren Xin	九天 (Jiǔ Tiān) 天冲 (Tiān Chōng) 惊门 (Jīng Mén) Kun 2 Wu Ji/Bing
太阴 (Tài Yīn) O 天心 (Tiān Xīn) 杜门 (Dù Mén) Zhen 3 Ding Wu	YinDun#3 Hour: XinHai ©Calvin Yap	九地 (Jiǔ Dì) 天辅 (Tiān Fǔ) 开门 (Kāi Mén) Dui 7 Yi Gui
六合 (Liù Hé) O 天柱 (Tiān Zhù) 伤门 (Shāng Mén) Gen 8 Gui Ren	白虎 (Bái Hǔ) 禽芮 (Qín Ruì) 生门 (Shēng Mén) Kan 1 Ji/Bing Geng	玄武 (Xuán Wǔ) 天英 (Tiān Yīng) 休门 (Xiū Mén) Qian 6 Xin Ding

Analysis

She was asking about her house Fengshui. So, matter asked is represented by Hour Heavenly Stem Xin which is at Qian 6 Palace. In Qian 6 Palace, there is 玄武 (Xuán Wǔ), 天英 (Tiān Yīng) and 休门 (Xiū Mén). With 玄武 (Xuán Wǔ) means the house had "funny things" happening.

At the East sector of the house, we looked at Zhen 3 Palace and there is 太阴 (Tài Yīn). 太阴 (Tài Yīn) means spirit and with 杜门 (Dù Mén) means that a spirit could be stuck there.

She didn't believe at first but a few months later, her husband's friend who is a medium, went to visit them. Her husband's friend told them that there was an old woman's spirit living in the house.

Case 10: Girlfriend left him

Background

I received an email from a friend saying that his girlfriend had left him. I plotted a Qi Men Dun Jia chart and told him that their relationship was already having problems and she left him for someone else.

The date and time when question asked was on: 5th December 2011 at 15:30

The chart is as follow:

Hour	Day	Month	Year
Ren	Jia	Ji	Xin
Shen	Wu	Hai	Mao

Yong Shen for relationship

YinDun#5 Hour: **RenShen** ; 直符(ZhíFú): **天禽(Tiān Qín)** ; 直使(ZhíShǐ): **死门 (Sǐ Mén)** ; 旬首(XúnShǒu): **JiaZiWu**

玄武 (Xuán Wǔ) 天蓬 (Tiān Péng) 生门 (Shēng Mén) Xun 4 Ren Ji	白虎 (Bái Hǔ) 天任 (Tiān Rèn) 伤门 (Shāng Mén) Li 9 Ding Gui	六合 (Liù Hé) 天冲 (Tiān Chōng) 杜门 (Dù Mén) Kun 2 Geng Xin/Wu
九地 (Jiǔ Dì) 天心 (Tiān Xīn) 休门 (Xiū Mén) Zhen 3 Yi Geng	YinDun#5 Hour: RenShen ©Calvin Yap	太阴 (Tài Yīn) 天辅 (Tiān Fǔ) 景门 (Jǐng Mén) Dui 7 Ji Bing
九天 (Jiǔ Tiān) 马 天柱 (Tiān Zhù) 开门 (Kāi Mén) Gen 8 Bing Ding	值符 (Zhí Fú) 禽芮 (Qín Ruì) 惊门 (Jīng Mén) Kan 1 Xin/Wu Ren	螣蛇 (Téng Shé) O 天英 (Tiān Yīng) 死门 (Sǐ Mén) Qian 6 Gui Yi

Analysis

The Yong Shen (Useful God) for relationship is 六合 (Liù Hé) which is at Kun 2 Palace with 天冲 (Tiān Chōng) and 杜门 (Dù Mén). That's mean the relationship has problem as 天冲 (Tiān Chōng) means there are clashes and 杜门 (Dù Mén) means stuck. Hence, relationship was stuck.

Representing his girlfriend is Ji which is at Dui 7 Palace. Below Ji, there is Bing, which represents 3rd party male. As such, I told him that she left him for someone else.

Case 11: Project having problem, take action

Background

One of my students was delivering a project and did a divination on whether they were able to deliver it successfully.

The date and time when question asked was on: 5th May 2014 at 17:00

The chart is as follow:

Hour	Day	Month	Year
Ding	Bing	Wu	Jia
You	Zi	Chen	Wu

YangDun#8 Hour: **DingYou** ; 直符(ZhíFú): **天芮 (Tiān Ruì)** ;
直使(ZhíShǐ): **死门 (Sǐ Mén)** ; 旬首(XúnShǒu): **JiaWuXin**

九地 (Jiǔ Dì) O 天辅 (Tiān Fǔ) 杜门 (Dù Mén) Xun 4 Gui Gui	九天 (Jiǔ Tiān) 天英 (Tiān Yīng) 景门 (Jǐng Mén) Li 9 Ji Ji	值符 (Zhí Fú) 禽芮 (Qín Ruì) 死门 (Sǐ Mén) Kun 2 Xin/Ding Xin/Ding
玄武 (Xuán Wǔ) 天冲 (Tiān Chōng) 伤门 (Shāng Mén) Zhen 3 Ren Ren	YangDun#8 Hour: DingYou **Fu Yin** ©Calvin Yap	螣蛇 (Téng Shé) 天柱 (Tiān Zhù) 惊门 (Jīng Mén) Dui 7 Yi Yi
白虎 (Bái Hǔ) 天任 (Tiān Rèn) 生门 (Shēng Mén) Gen 8 Wu Wu	六合 (Liù Hé) 天蓬 (Tiān Péng) 休门 (Xiū Mén) Kan 1 Geng Geng	太阴 (Tài Yīn) 马 天心 (Tiān Xīn) 开门 (Kāi Mén) Qian 6 Bing Bing

Analysis

This is a Fu Yin chart. Hence, any matter asked would not be successful. The outcome would be stagnant. As such, I advised my student to change strategy and try to engage the client again.

A few months later, my student wrote to me saying that the project was completed and managed to get a compliment letter from the client. My student said that initially the client was very bad and kept on finding fault with the project. My student managed to engage another manager to help and managed to negotiate and pull through the project.

So, if my student had continued to engage the original manager, the project would fail. However, my student decided to take action and engaged another manager instead.

Case 12: Parents' volunteer interview

Background

One of my friends went for Parents Volunteer Interview. In Singapore, to ensure that you were given priority for your child to enter certain school, parents had to volunteer at that particular school. Parents usually had to go through interview session before they were selected.

So, my friend called me and asked me to do a divination on whether his selection will be successful. He was born in Jia Yin year.

The date and time when question asked was on: 7th March 2014 at 11:00

The chart is as follow:

Hour	Day	Month	Year
Bing	Ding	Ding	Jia
Wu	Chou	Mao	Wu

Using Birth Year, Gui to analyse

YangDun#4 Hour: **BingWu** ; 直符(ZhíFú): **天任 (Tiān Rèn)** ;
直使(ZhíShǐ): **生门 (Shēng Mén)** ; 旬首(XúnShǒu): **JiaChenRen**

九地 (Jiǔ Dì) 天心 (Tiān Xīn) 景门 (Jǐng Mén) Xun 4 Geng Wu	九天 (Jiǔ Tiān) 天蓬 (Tiān Péng) 死门 (Sǐ Mén) Li 9 Ding Gui	值符(Zhí Fú) 马 天任 (Tiān Rèn) 惊门 (Jīng Mén) Kun 2 Ren Bing/Ji
玄武 (Xuán Wǔ) O 天柱 (Tiān Zhù) 杜门 (Dù Mén) Zhen 3 Xin Yi	YangDun#4 Hour: BingWu **Fan Yin** ©Calvin Yap	螣蛇 (Téng Shé) 天冲 (Tiān Chōng) 开门 (Kāi Mén) Dui 7 Yi Xin
白虎 (Bái Hǔ) O 禽芮 (Qín Ruì) 伤门 (Shāng Mén) Gen 8 Bing/Ji Ren	六合 (Liù Hé) 天英 (Tiān Yīng) 生门 (Shēng Mén) Kan 1 Gui Ding	太阴 (Tài Yīn) 天辅 (Tiān Fǔ) 休门 (Xiū Mén) Qian 6 Wu Geng

Analysis

He was born in Jia Yin Year, so we use Gui. Gui is at Kan 1 Palace with 六合 (Liù Hé), 天英 (Tiān Yīng) and 生门 (Shēng Mén). Interviewer is represented by 天辅 (Tiān Fǔ) at Qian 6 Palace and it's in giving birth situation with Gui, which represents my friend. Based on the analysis, his interview should be successful.

Looking at the chart, Day Heavenly Stem represents all the parents going for interview. Day Heavenly Stem is Ding which is at Li 9 Palace with 死门 (Sǐ Mén) and 天蓬 (Tiān Péng). 天蓬 (Tiān Péng) means robber so, they are trying to out-do each other by robbing for opportunity.

He told me that he had successfully secured the role as a parent volunteer. He said that the interview was tense and competitive because every parents were trying to out-do each other.

Case 13: Relationship

Background

One lady came for consult and asked about her relationship. I plotted a Qi Men Dun Jia chart and told her that her husband was having an affair. She was shocked with the accuracy of reading.

The date and time when question asked was on: 9th Feb 2010 at 12:00

The chart is as follow:

Hour	Day	Month	Year
Ren	Geng	Wu	Geng
Wu	Yin	Yin	Yin

YangDun#2 Hour: **RenWu** ; 直符(ZhíFú): **天冲 (Tiān Chōng)** ;
直使(ZhíShǐ): **伤门 (Shāng Mén)** ; 旬首(XúnShǒu): **JiaXuJi**

白虎 (Bái Hǔ) 天柱 (Tiān Zhù) 休门 (Xiū Mén) Xun 4 Gui Geng	玄武 (Xuán Wǔ) 天心 (Tiān Xīn) 生门 (Shēng Mén) Li 9 Ren Bing	九地 (Jiǔ Dì) O 马 天蓬 (Tiān Péng) 伤门 (Shāng Mén) Kun 2 Yi Wu/Xin
六合 (Liù Hé) 禽芮 (Qín Ruì) 开门 (Kāi Mén) Zhen 3 Wu/Xin Ji	YangDun#2 Hour: RenWu ©Calvin Yap	九天 (Jiǔ Tiān) O 天任 (Tiān Rèn) 杜门 (Dù Mén) Dui 7 Ding Gui
太阴 (Tài Yīn) 天英 (Tiān Yīng) 惊门 (Jīng Mén) Gen 8 Bing Ding	腾蛇 (Téng Shé) 天辅 (Tiān Fǔ) 死门 (Sǐ Mén) Kan 1 Geng Yi	值符 (Zhí Fú) 天冲 (Tiān Chōng) 景门 (Jǐng Mén) Qian 6 Ji Ren

Yong Shen for relationship

Analysis

Day Heavenly Stem represents the person asking. Day Heavenly Stem is Geng which is at Kan 1 Palace with 死门 (Sǐ Mén) and 螣蛇 (Téng Shé). So she was in bad luck and was vexed. Representing her husband is Yi which is at Kun 2 Palace with Kong and Horse. That's mean her husband might have left her or was already not around.

Besides, Geng and Yi are at different Pan so they were already separated.

Representing marriage is 六合 (Liù Hé) which is at Zhen 3 Palace. With 天芮 (Tiān Ruì), this means her marriage has problem. In addition, there is 开门 (Kāi Mén) and this means her marriage is open for 3rd party to come in.

Representing 3rd party (husband mistress) is Ding which is at Dui 7 Palace. It is in giving birth situation with her husband at Kun 2 Palace. As such, I predicted her husband had an affair and already left her.

Bazi Cases

Breast Cancer Indicator

Angelina Jolie decided to perform double mastectomy to prevent breast cancer. It had shocked the world as she had her breasts removed not because she has cancer but as precaution measure to prevent from getting cancer. The actress has a defective gene, BRCA1, which significantly increases her risk of developing breast cancer and ovarian cancer. The latter disease killed her mother at the age of 56.

According to The Guardian, women with a defect in BRCA1 have on average a 65% risk of developing breast cancer. Jolie said her doctors told her that her risk was 87% and that surgery had reduced it to 5%. The defect also increases the risk of ovarian cancer, which Jolie said doctor's estimattion for her is 50%.

This really stirs up the discussion in the Asia world. Most of the doctors in Singapore actually don't recommend mastectomy until it is necessary.

I remembered my Master once told me a couple of years ago that Breast Cancer can be seen as indicator in a Bazi chart. So, I am sharing this information to the general public so that they are well-informed and to take whatever measures needed. Just note that having such indicator in a Bazi does not mean that you will have Breast Cancer. It only put you in the higher risk group. In addition, there are also other factors that require further analysis. For example, the Fengshui of your house - whether it supports the sickness or support the curing of sickness. Timing is another factor that needs to be taken into consideration. This is when the sickness can be detected. Like what's being reported, having a defect BRCA1 does not mean you will develop Breast Cancer; it only increases the chances.

In Qi Men Dun Jia, the Zhen 3 Palace and Dui 7 Palace represent left and right breast respectively. If there is Geng or Xin in either or both palaces, then it indicates that there is potential growth in those areas. The worst case is when there is 天芮 (Tiān Ruì) star residing in either Zhen 3 or Dui 7 palace.

Case 14: Sheryl Crow (diagnosed on 2006 at age 44)

"I am a walking advertisement for early detection," Sheryl Crow said in October 2006 about catching suspicious calcifications in both of her breasts on a routine mammogram. The rocker immediately postponed a tour, went into surgery, and had seven weeks of radiation, supplemented with acupuncture and herbal teas. Crow—whose engagement to cyclist Lance Armstrong ended around the time she was diagnosed—was able to skip chemotherapy because her cancer was caught so early. In March 2007, Crow (who has no close family history of breast cancer) petitioned Congress to fund research into possible links between breast cancer and environmental factors.

Source: http://www.health.com/health/gallery/0,,20307103_2,00.html

Date and time of birth: 11ᵗʰ Feb 1962 at 09:58 (Source: Astro Databank)

The chart is as follow:

Hour	Day	Month	Year
Xin	Geng	Ren	Ren
Si	Chen	Yin	Yin

Tian Rui = Sickness

YangDun#8 Hour: **XinSi** ; 直符(ZhíFú): **天英 (Tiān Yīng)** ;
直使(ZhíShǐ): **景门 (Jǐng Mén)** ; 旬首(XúnShǒu): **JiaXuJi**

九地 (Jiǔ Dì) 天冲 (Tiān Chōng) 生门 (Shēng Mén) Xun 4 Ren Gui	九天 (Jiǔ Tiān) 天辅 (Tiān Fǔ) 伤门 (Shāng Mén) Li 9 Gui Ji	值符 (Zhí Fú) O 天英 (Tiān Yīng) 杜门 (Dù Mén) Kun 2 Ji Xin/Ding
玄武 (Xuán Wǔ) 天任 (Tiān Rèn) 休门 (Xiū Mén) Zhen 3 Wu Ren	YangDun#8 Hour: XinSi ©Calvin Yap	螣蛇 (Téng Shé) O 禽芮 (Qín Ruì) 景门 (Jǐng Mén) Dui 7 Xin/Ding Yi
白虎 (Bái Hǔ) 天蓬 (Tiān Péng) 开门 (Kāi Mén) Gen 8 Geng Wu	六合 (Liù Hé) 天心 (Tiān Xīn) 惊门 (Jīng Mén) Kan 1 Bing Geng	太阴 (Tài Yīn) 马 天柱 (Tiān Zhù) 死门 (Sǐ Mén) Qian 6 Yi Bing

Analysis

Yong Shen (Useful God) for sickness is 天芮 (Tiān Ruì) which is at Dui 7 Palace. For woman, Dui 7 Palace represents left breast. In Dui 7 Palace there is Xin, which represents small growth.

She was diagnosed in 2006, which is Bing Xu year. However, I believed that her problem could have started in 2005, Ding You year. This was because You Earthly Branch is at Dui 7 palace, that's where the Kong would be filled up during that year.

Case 15: Kylie Minogue (diagnosed 2005 at 36)

A misdiagnosis almost lost Australian pop star Kylie Minogue her chance to fight—and defeat—breast cancer. It wasn't until she decided to go in for a second round of tests that doctors found the lump in her left breast. A partial mastectomy, chemotherapy, and radiation followed.

The singer has emerged from her ordeal with a plea that women should trust their gut more when they go to the doctor. "Just because someone is in a white coat and using big medical instruments doesn't necessarily mean they're right," she told Ellen DeGeneres in 2007.

Source: http://www.health.com/health/gallery/0,,20307103_4,00.html

Date and time of birth: 28th May 1968 at 11:16 (Source: Astro Databank)

The chart is as follow:

Hour	Day	Month	Year
Wu	Wu	Ding	Wu
Wu	Xu	Si	Shen

Tian Rui = Sickness

YangDun#5 Hour: **WuWu** ; 直符(ZhíFú): **天蓬 (Tiān Péng)** ;
直使(ZhíShǐ): **休门 (Xiū Mén)** ; 旬首(XúnShǒu): **JiaYinGui**

九地 (Jiǔ Dì) 天柱 (Tiān Zhù) 惊门 (Jīng Mén) Xun 4 Geng Yi	九天 (Jiǔ Tiān) 天心 (Tiān Xīn) 开门 (Kāi Mén) Li 9 Ji Ren	值符 (Zhí Fú) 马 天蓬 (Tiān Péng) 休门 (Xiū Mén) Kun 2 Gui Ding/Wu
玄武 (Xuán Wǔ) 禽芮 (Qín Ruì) 死门 (Sǐ Mén) Zhen 3 Ding/Wu Bing	YangDun#5 Hour: WuWu ©Calvin Yap	螣蛇 (Téng Shé) 天任 (Tiān Rèn) 生门 (Shēng Mén) Dui 7 Xin Geng
白虎 (Bái Hǔ) O 天英 (Tiān Yīng) 景门 (Jǐng Mén) Gen 8 Ren Xin	六合 (Liù Hé) O 天辅 (Tiān Fǔ) 杜门 (Dù Mén) Kan 1 Yi Gui	太阴 (Tài Yīn) 天冲 (Tiān Chōng) 伤门 (Shāng Mén) Qian 6 Bing Ji

Analysis

Yong Shen (Useful God) for sickness is 天芮 (Tiān Ruì) which is at Zhen 3 Palace. For woman, Zhen 3 Palace represents left breast. Looking at Dui 7 palace, there are Xin and Geng residing in this palace. Xin and Geng are indicators for growth.

She was diagnosed in 2005, Ding You year. Ding is at Zhen 3 Palace together with her Day Master, Wu. While, You is at Dui 7 Palace clashing with Zhen 3 Palace.

Case 16: Christina Applegate (diagnosed 2008 at 36)

For most women, the idea of parting with one breast, let alone two, is unimaginable. But that's what actress Christina Applegate opted to do after she was diagnosed with breast cancer in the summer of 2008, even though cancer was found in only one breast.

Applegate—who tested positive for the BRCA-1 gene mutation and whose mother is a repeat breast cancer survivor—said she chose mastectomy to reduce the chance that the cancer could spread or come back. Applegate later founded Right Action for Women, a nonprofit that provides financial aid to women at high risk of breast cancer.

Source: http://www.health.com/health/gallery/0,,20307103_8,00.html

Date and time of birth: 25th November 1971 at 17:45 (Source: Astro Databank)

The chart is as follow:

Hour	Day	Month	Year
Gui	Jia	Ji	Xin
You	Yin	Hai	Hai

Tian Rui = Sickness

YinDun#8 Hour: **GuiYou** ; 直符(ZhíFú): **天任 (Tiān Rèn)** ; 直使(ZhíShǐ): **生门 (Shēng Mén)** ; 旬首(XúnShǒu): **JiaZiWu**

九天 (Jiǔ Tiān) 天冲 (Tiān Chōng) 杜门 (Dù Mén) Xun 4 Gui Ren	九地 (Jiǔ Dì) 天辅 (Tiān Fǔ) 景门 (Jǐng Mén) Li 9 Ren Yi	玄武 (Xuán Wǔ) 天英 (Tiān Yīng) 死门 (Sǐ Mén) Kun 2 Yi Ding/Xin
值符 (Zhí Fú) 天任 (Tiān Rèn) 伤门 (Shāng Mén) Zhen 3 Wu Gui	YinDun#8 Hour: GuiYou ©Calvin Yap	白虎 (Bái Hǔ) 禽芮 (Qín Ruì) 惊门 (Jīng Mén) Dui 7 Ding/Xin Ji
腾蛇 (Téng Shé) 天蓬 (Tiān Péng) 生门 (Shēng Mén) Gen 8 Bing Wu	太阴 (Tài Yīn) 天心 (Tiān Xīn) 休门 (Xiū Mén) Kan 1 Geng Bing	六合 (Liù Hé) **O 马** 天柱 (Tiān Zhù) 开门 (Kāi Mén) Qian 6 Ji Geng

Analysis

Yong Shen (Useful God) for sickness is 天芮 (Tiān Ruì) which is at Dui 7 Palace. For woman, Dui 7 Palace represents right breast. In the same palace, there is Xin which is an indicator for growth.

She was diagnosed in 2008, Wu Zi year. Wu is at Zhen 3 Palace clashing with Dui 7 Palace where 天芮 (Tiān Ruì) sickness star is.

Case 17: Judy Holliday

Judy Holliday (June 21, 1921 – June 7, 1965) was an American actress, comedian and singer.

She began her career as part of a nightclub act before working in Broadway plays and musicals. Her success in the 1946 stage production of Born Yesterday as "Billie Dawn" led to her being cast in the 1950 film version for which she won an Academy Award for Best Actress and a Golden Globe Award for Best Actress - Motion Picture Musical or Comedy. She appeared regularly in films during the 1950s. She was noted for her performance on Broadway in the musical Bells Are Ringing, winning a Tony Award for Best Performance by a Leading Actress in a Musical and reprising her role in the 1960 film.

She died from breast cancer on June 7, 1965, aged 43

Source: http://en.wikipedia.org/wiki/Judy_Holliday

Date and time of birth: 21st June 1921 at 23:40 (Source: Astro Databank)

The chart is as follow:

Hour	Day	Month	Year
Wu	Bing	Jia	Xin
Zi	Chen	Wu	You

Tian Rui = Sickness

YangDun#3 Hour: **WuZi** ; 直符(ZhíFú): 天禽(**Tiān Qín**) ;
直使(ZhíShǐ): 死门 (**Sǐ Mén**) ; 旬首(XúnShǒu): **JiaShenGeng**

螣蛇 (Téng Shé) 天柱 (Tiān Zhù) 景门 (Jǐng Mén) Xun 4 Ren Ji	太阴 (Tài Yīn) O 天心 (Tiān Xīn) 死门 (Sǐ Mén) Li 9 Xin Ding	六合 (Liù Hé) O 天蓬 (Tiān Péng) 惊门 (Jīng Mén) Kun 2 Bing Yi/Geng
值符 (Zhí Fú) 禽芮 (Qín Ruì) 杜门 (Dù Mén) Zhen 3 Yi/Geng Wu	YangDun#3 Hour: WuZi ©Calvin Yap	白虎 (Bái Hǔ) 天任 (Tiān Rèn) 开门 (Kāi Mén) Dui 7 Gui Ren
九天 (Jiǔ Tiān) 马 天英 (Tiān Yīng) 伤门 (Shāng Mén) Gen 8 Ding Gui	九地 (Jiǔ Dì) 天辅 (Tiān Fǔ) 生门 (Shēng Mén) Kan 1 Ji Bing	玄武 (Xuán Wǔ) 天冲 (Tiān Chōng) 休门 (Xiū Mén) Qian 6 Wu Xin

Analysis

Yong Shen (Useful God) for sickness is 天芮 (Tiān Ruì) which is at Zhen 3 Palace. By now we already know that for woman, Zhen 3 Palace represents left breast. In the same palace, we could see that there is Geng and it is an indicator for growth.

Case 18: Angelina Jolie

On February 16, 2013, at the age of 37, Jolie underwent a preventive double mastectomy after learning she had an 87% risk of developing breast cancer due to a defective BRCA1 gene. Her family history warranted genetic testing for BRCA mutations: her mother, actress Marcheline Bertrand, had breast cancer and died from ovarian cancer in 2007 at the age of 56, while her maternal grandmother had ovarian cancer and died aged 45. Her maternal aunt Debbie Martin, who had the same defective BRCA1 gene as Jolie, was diagnosed with breast cancer in 2004 and died at age 61 on May 26, 2013. Jolie's mastectomy lowered her chances of developing breast cancer to under 5 percent, and testing of the removed breast tissue showed no signs of cancerous cells. On April 27, Jolie had reconstructive surgery involving implants and allografts (transplants). She reportedly intends to undergo a preventive oophorectomy (ovariectomy), as she still has a 50% risk of developing ovarian cancer due to the same genetic anomaly.

Source: http://en.wikipedia.org/wiki/Angelina_Jolie

Date and time of birth: 4th June 1975 at 09:09 (Source: Astro Databank)

The chart is as follow:

Hour	Day	Month	Year
Gui	Xin	Xin	Yi
Si	Si	Si	Mao

YangDun#5 Hour: **GuiSi** ; 直符(ZhíFú): **天柱 (Tiān Zhù)** ;
直使(ZhíShǐ): **惊门 (Jīng Mén)** ; 旬首(XúnShǒu): **JiaShenGeng**

六合 (Liù Hé) 天任 (Tiān Rèn) 杜门 (Dù Mén) Xun 4 Xin Yi	白虎 (Bái Hǔ) O 天冲 (Tiān Chōng) 景门 (Jǐng Mén) Li 9 Bing Ren	玄武 (Xuán Wǔ) O 天辅 (Tiān Fǔ) 死门 (Sǐ Mén) Kun 2 Yi Ding/Wu
太阴 (Tài Yīn) 天蓬 (Tiān Péng) 伤门 (Shāng Mén) Zhen 3 Gui Bing	YangDun#5 Hour: GuiSi ©Calvin Yap	九地 (Jiǔ Dì) 天英 (Tiān Yīng) 惊门 (Jīng Mén) Dui 7 Ren Geng
螣蛇 (Téng Shé) 天心 (Tiān Xīn) 生门 (Shēng Mén) Gen 8 Ji Xin	值符 (Zhí Fú) 天柱 (Tiān Zhù) 休门 (Xiū Mén) Kan 1 Geng Gui	九天 (Jiǔ Tiān) 马 禽芮 (Qín Ruì) 开门 (Kāi Mén) Qian 6 Ding/Wu Ji

Analysis

Although her 天芮 (Tiān Ruì) is not residing in either Zhen 3 or Dui 7 Palace, however, she has a Di Pan Geng at Dui 7 Palace. Hence, there are still chances that she might get growth at her breast.

Looking at Kan 1 Palace, which represents ovary for woman, there is Geng. Therefore, her chances of having ovary growth are higher.

Breast Cancer Indicator – note

Please note the following: having Geng and Xin with 天芮 (Tiān Ruì) at Zhen 3 or Dui 7 Palace doesn't mean you will have breast cancer. However, prevention is always better than cure. So, for women who have Geng and Xin with 天芮 (Tiān Ruì) residing in either Zhen 3 or Dui 7 Palace, you are recommended to go for regular checkup.

Please check with your doctor on the possibility of having regular checkup.

Ability to connect with the supernatural

There are cases where people claimed that they are able to connect with the supernatural or spiritually inclined. This can be seen by using Qi Men Dun Jia Bazi. Below are some examples of people with such capability.

Case 19: Date of Birth: 7th Dec 2007 at Xu hour

The chart is as follow:

Hour	Day	Month	Year
Bing	Yi	Ren	Ding
Xu	Hai	Zi	Hai

YinDun#2 Hour: **BingXu** ; 直符(ZhíFú): **天英 (Tiān Yīng)** ;
直使(ZhíShǐ): **景门 (Jǐng Mén)** ; 旬首(XúnShǒu): **JiaShenGeng**

值符 (Zhí Fú) 天英 (Tiān Yīng) 生门 (Shēng Mén) Xun 4 Geng Bing	九天 (Jiǔ Tiān) O 禽芮 (Qín Ruì) 伤门 (Shāng Mén) Li 9 Wu/Ding Geng	九地 (Jiǔ Dì) O 马 天柱 (Tiān Zhù) 杜门 (Dù Mén) Kun 2 Ren Wu/Ding
螣蛇 (Téng Shé) 天辅 (Tiān Fǔ) 休门 (Xiū Mén) Zhen 3 Bing Yi	YinDun#2 Hour: BingXu ©Calvin Yap	玄武 (Xuán Wǔ) 天心 (Tiān Xīn) 景门 (Jǐng Mén) Dui 7 Gui Ren
太阴 (Tài Yīn) 天冲 (Tiān Chōng) 开门 (Kāi Mén) Gen 8 Yi Xin	六合 (Liù Hé) 天任 (Tiān Rèn) 惊门 (Jīng Mén) Kan 1 Xin Ji	白虎 (Bái Hǔ) 天蓬 (Tiān Péng) 死门 (Sǐ Mén) Qian 6 Ji Gui

Analysis

We looked at Gen 8 palace, where the Day Master Tian Pan Yi is residing. Together in the same palace, there is 太阴 (Tài Yīn) which represents spiritual or have the ability to connect with the supernatural.

Case 20: Date of Birth: 22nd Mar 2013 at 06:53

The chart is as follow:

Hour	Day	Month	Year
Gui	Ding	Yi	Gui
Mao	Hai	Mao	Si

YangDun#9 Hour: **GuiMao** ; 直符(ZhíFú): **天冲 (Tiān Chōng)** ; 直使(ZhíShǐ): **伤门 (Shāng Mén)** ; 旬首(XúnShǒu): **JiaWuXin**

九地 (Jiǔ Dì) O 马 天蓬 (Tiān Péng) 杜门 (Dù Mén) Xun 4 Ji Ren	九天 (Jiǔ Tiān) 天任 (Tiān Rèn) 景门 (Jǐng Mén) Li 9 Yi Wu	值符 (Zhí Fú) 天冲 (Tiān Chōng) 死门 (Sǐ Mén) Kun 2 Xin Geng/Gui
玄武 (Xuán Wǔ) 天心 (Tiān Xīn) 伤门 (Shāng Mén) Zhen 3 Ding Xin	YangDun#9 Hour: GuiMao ©Calvin Yap	螣蛇 (Téng Shé) 天辅 (Tiān Fǔ) 惊门 (Jīng Mén) Dui 7 Ren Bing
白虎 (Bái Hǔ) 天柱 (Tiān Zhù) 生门 (Shēng Mén) Gen 8 Bing Yi	六合 (Liù Hé) 禽芮 (Qín Ruì) 休门 (Xiū Mén) Kan 1 Geng/Gui Ji	太阴 (Tài Yīn) 天英 (Tiān Yīng) 开门 (Kāi Mén) Qian 6 Wu Ding

Analysis

Apart from looking at Day Heavenly Stem Tian Pan, we can also look at Day Heavenly Stem Di Pan. In this case, Day Heavenly Stem Di Pan is Ding which is at Qian 6 Palace. In that same palace, there is 太阴 (Tài Yīn) which represents spiritual or have the ability to connect with the supernatural.

Case 21: Nella Jones's Date of Birth 4th May 1932 at 10:30

The chart is as follow:

Hour	Day	Month	Year
Xin	Yi	Jia	Ren
Si	Chou	Chen	Shen

YangDun#5 Hour: **XinSi** ; 直符(ZhíFú): **天心 (Tiān Xīn)** ; 直使(ZhíShǐ): **开门 (Kāi Mén)** ; 旬首(XúnShǒu): **JiaXuJi**

太阴 (Tài Yīn) 天任 (Tiān Rèn) 开门 (Kāi Mén) Xun 4 Xin Yi	六合 (Liù Hé) 天冲 (Tiān Chōng) 休门 (Xiū Mén) Li 9 Bing Ren	白虎 (Bái Hǔ) O 天辅 (Tiān Fǔ) 生门 (Shēng Mén) Kun 2 Yi Ding/Wu
螣蛇 (Téng Shé) 天蓬 (Tiān Péng) 惊门 (Jīng Mén) Zhen 3 Gui Bing	YangDun#5 Hour: XinSi ©Calvin Yap	玄武 (Xuán Wǔ) O 天英 (Tiān Yīng) 伤门 (Shāng Mén) Dui 7 Ren Geng
值符 (Zhí Fú) 天心 (Tiān Xīn) 死门 (Sǐ Mén) Gen 8 Ji Xin	九天 (Jiǔ Tiān) 天柱 (Tiān Zhù) 景门 (Jǐng Mén) Kan 1 Geng Gui	九地 (Jiǔ Dì) 马 禽芮 (Qín Ruì) 杜门 (Dù Mén) Qian 6 Ding/Wu Ji

Analysis

In the above bazi, we look at Day Heavenly Stem Di Pan Yi which is residing in Xun 4 Palace. In that same palace there is 太阴 (Tài Yīn) which means she has the ability to connect with the supernatural or is spiritually incline.

Case 22: Lady Diana - At the wrong place, at the wrong time.

British royalty, daughter of the 8th Earl of Spencer with excellent lineage that dates back to the 15th century, the 11th cousin once removed to Prince Charles, heir to the throne of the U.K.

Date and time of birth: 1st **July 1961 at 19:45** (Source: Astro Databank)

The chart is as follow:

Hour	Day	Month	Year
Bing	Yi	Jia	Xin
Xu	Wei	Wu	Chou

YinDun#9 Hour: **BingXu** ; 直符(ZhíFú): **天柱 (Tiān Zhù)** ;
直使(ZhíShǐ): **惊门 (Jīng Mén)** ; 旬首(XúnShǒu): **JiaShenGeng**

太阴 (Tài Yīn) 天英 (Tiān Yīng) 景门 (Jǐng Mén) Xun 4 Wu Gui	螣蛇 (Téng Shé) O 禽芮 (Qín Ruì) 死门 (Sǐ Mén) Li 9 Bing Wu	值符 (Zhí Fú) O 马 天柱 (Tiān Zhù) 惊门 (Jīng Mén) Kun 2 Geng Bing/Ren
六合 (Liù Hé) 天辅 (Tiān Fǔ) 杜门 (Dù Mén) Zhen 3 Gui Ding	YinDun#9 Hour: BingXu ©Calvin Yap	九天 (Jiǔ Tiān) 天心 (Tiān Xīn) 开门 (Kāi Mén) Dui 7 Xin Geng
白虎 (Bái Hǔ) 天冲 (Tiān Chōng) 伤门 (Shāng Mén) Gen 8 Ding Ji	玄武 (Xuán Wǔ) 天仟 (Tiān Rèn) 生门 (Shēng Mén) Kan 1 Ji Yi	九地 (Jiǔ Dì) 天蓬 (Tiān Péng) 休门 (Xiū Mén) Qian 6 Yi Xin

Analysis

Her Day Master is Yi which is at Qian 6 Palace, while her husband is Geng which is at Kun 2 Palace. In Kun 2 Palace, there is Kong and Horse.

In November 1980 (Geng Shen), she met Prince Charles, whom she already idolized. In 1980 which is Geng Shen year, with Geng Heavenly Stem and Shen Earthly Branch both residing in Kun 2 Palace, that year it fills up the Kong in Kun 2 palace. Thus, her potential husband appeared. Her potential husband is a leader (prince) because in Kun 2 Palace, there is 值符 (Zhí Fú) which represents leader.

After five months of engagement, they married at St. Paul's Cathedral on 29th July 1981 at 11:17:30 AM. 1981 is Xin You year; both Xin Heavenly Stem and You Earthly Branch are in Dui 7 Palace. Opposite Dui 7 palace is Zhen 3 Palace. In Zhen 3 Palace, there is 六合 (Liù Hé) which respresents relationship and it was being clashed by Dui 7 Palace. When 六合 (Liù Hé) is being clashed, this would mean there will be movement in relationship. Hence, she got married in 1981 (Xin You).

On 31st Aug 1997 at 00:25 AM, Diana and Dodi were involved in a car accident in a tunnel along the river Seine in Paris. When French emergency services arrived, they pronounced Al Fayad dead. Doctors attempted to revive Diana at 00:35 AM. It took 52 minutes to extricate her from the mangled car and transported her four miles to Pitie-Saletriere Hospital, where they arrived at 2:05 AM. Diana's heart had stopped beating at 1:50 AM. Doctors stopped their efforts to revive her at 3:45 AM and she was officially pronounced dead at 4:07AM. Had she and Dodi been wearing their seat belts, they would have survived.

1997 is Ding Chou Year. Looking at her Qi Men Dun Jia Bazi, Ding and Chou both were residing in Gen 8 Palace with 白虎 (Bái Hǔ), 天冲 (Tiān Chōng) and 伤门 (Shāng Mén). 伤门 (Shāng Mén) represents transportation and in this case, car. 天冲 (Tiān Chōng) represents clash and together with 伤门 (Shāng Mén) would mean car crash. In addition there is 白虎 (Bái Hǔ) which means ferociously car accident.

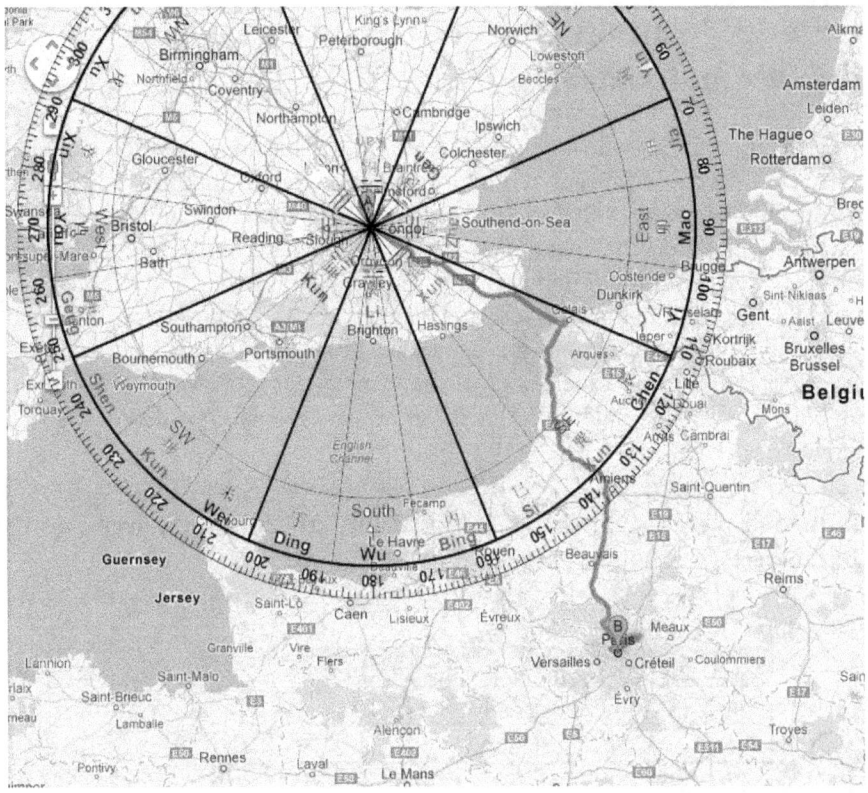

On the day of accident, she was at the SE sector (Xun 4 Palace) from her house. Her SE sector is her 景门 (Jǐng Mén) which represents blood related calamity. It clashed her Day Master Yi which is at Qian 6 Palace.

Case 23: Whitney Houston - House Fengshui doesn't match her bazi.

American pop diva with a three octave range, a spectacular video and film actress. A precocious beauty with virtuosity and lyrical authority, she began a carefully planned career in 1981 with TV commercials and guest spots. She also modeled in Glamour and Vogue and sang club dates with her mother, Cissy. With her debut album, Houston sold over 18 million copies world wide. She has surpassed the Beatles in consecutive No.1 hits and been the recipient of Grammy's, American Music Awards, People's Choice Awards, Emmys and Entertainer of the Year given by NAACP. Described as an extraordinary talent, ethereal yet warm, she is considered a gifted singer.

Date and time of birth: 9th Aug 1963 at 20:55 (Source: Astro Databank)

The chart is as follow:

Hour	Day	Month	Year
Jia	Jia	Geng	Gui
Xu	Shen	Shen	Mao

YinDun#5 Hour: **JiaXu** ; 直符(ZhíFú): **天辅 (Tiān Fǔ)** ; 直使(ZhíShǐ): **杜门 (Dù Mén)** ; 旬首(XúnShǒu): **JiaXuJi**

值符 (Zhí Fú) 天辅 (Tiān Fǔ) 杜门 (Dù Mén) Xun 4 Ji Ji	九天 (Jiǔ Tiān) 天英 (Tiān Yīng) 景门 (Jǐng Mén) Li 9 Gui Gui	九地 (Jiǔ Dì) O 马 禽芮 (Qín Ruì) 死门 (Sǐ Mén) Kun 2 Xin/Wu Xin/Wu
腾蛇 (Téng Shé) 天冲 (Tiān Chōng) 伤门 (Shāng Mén) Zhen 3 Geng Geng	YinDun#5 Hour: JiaXu **Fu Yin** ©Calvin Yap	玄武 (Xuán Wǔ) O 天柱 (Tiān Zhù) 惊门 (Jīng Mén) Dui 7 Bing Bing
太阴 (Tài Yīn) 天任 (Tiān Rèn) 生门 (Shēng Mén) Gen 8 Ding Ding	六合 (Liù Hé) 天蓬 (Tiān Péng) 休门 (Xiū Mén) Kan 1 Ren Ren	白虎 (Bái Hǔ) 天心 (Tiān Xīn) 开门 (Kāi Mén) Qian 6 Yi Yi

Her house when she died: 22 North Gate Road, in Mendham, N.J.

Source: http://blogs.westword.com/backbeat/2012/02/whitney_houston_new_jersey_mansion_for_sale.php

The house is sitting SW and Facing NE.

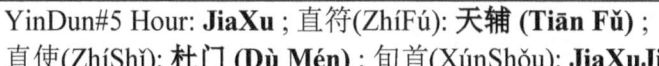

YinDun#5 Hour: **JiaXu** ; 直符(ZhíFú): **天辅 (Tiān Fǔ)** ; 直使(ZhíShǐ): **杜门 (Dù Mén)** ; 旬首(XúnShǒu): **JiaXuJi**		
值符 (Zhí Fú) 天辅 (Tiān Fǔ) 杜门 (Dù Mén) Xun 4 Ji Ji	九天 (Jiǔ Tiān) 天英 (Tiān Yīng) 景门 (Jǐng Mén) Li 9 Gui Gui	九地 (Jiǔ Dì) O 马 禽芮 (Qín Ruì) 死门 (Sǐ Mén) Kun 2 Xin/Wu Xin/Wu
螣蛇 (Téng Shé) 天冲 (Tiān Chōng) 伤门 (Shāng Mén) Zhen 3 Geng Geng	YinDun#5 Hour: JiaXu **Fu Yin** ©Calvin Yap	玄武 (Xuán Wǔ) O 天柱 (Tiān Zhù) 惊门 (Jīng Mén) Dui 7 Bing Bing
太阴 (Tài Yīn) 天任 (Tiān Rèn) 生门 (Shēng Mén) Gen 8 Ding Ding	六合 (Liù Hé) 天蓬 (Tiān Péng) 休门 (Xiū Mén) Kan 1 Ren Ren	白虎 (Bái Hǔ) 天心 (Tiān Xīn) 开门 (Kāi Mén) Qian 6 Yi Yi

Her house is sitting South West and by mapping that to her bazi, South West is where her 死门 (Sǐ Mén) resides. So, she was living in a house that was bad for her.

She died on 11th Feb 2012 around 3.55 pm in the Beverly Hills Hilton hotel, CA, at the age of 48. She was due to perform at a pre-Grammy award party in Los Angeles that evening. Police said her entourage had taken up a large part of the hotel's fourth floor. The autopsy report issued some weeks later stated that she drowned accidentally in the bathtub.

2012 is Ren Chen Year. In her Qi Men chart, Tai Sui Ren is at Kan 1 Palace, which is Water. Tai Sui Ren is in conflict with Kun 2 Palace which is Earth and Kun 2 Palace is her house is sitting and also where her 死门 (Sǐ Mén) is. As such, she died in 2012 as she could not use her house Fengshui to save her from the mishap.

Case 24: Michael Jordon - House Fengshui that helps his career.

Michael Jeffrey Jordan is a retired American professional basketball player and active businessman. . In 1991, he won his first NBA championship with the Bulls, and followed that achievement with titles in 1992 and 1993, securing a "three-peat." Jordan's second season was cut short by a broken foot which caused him to miss 64 games. Jordan had recovered completely by the 1986–87 season, and had one of the most prolific scoring seasons in NBA history. Though Jordan abruptly left the NBA at the beginning of the 1993-94 NBA season to pursue a career in baseball, he rejoined the Bulls in 1995 and led them to three additional championships (1996, 1997, and 1998) as well as an NBA-record 72 regular-season wins in the 1995–96 season. Jordan retired for a second time in 1999, but he returned for two more NBA seasons in 2001 as a member of the Washington Wizards.

Date and time of birth: 17th Feb 1963 at 16:30 (Source: Astro Databank)

The chart is as follow:

Hour	Day	Month	Year
Bing	Xin	Jia	Gui
Shen	Mao	Yin	Mao

YangDun#2 Hour: **BingShen** ; 直符(ZhíFú): **天禽(Tiān Qín)** ;
直使(ZhíShǐ): **死门 (Sǐ Mén)** ; 旬首(XúnShǒu): **JiaWuXin**

九天 (Jiǔ Tiān) O 天英 (Tiān Yīng) 伤门 (Shāng Mén) Xun 4 Bing Geng	值符 (Zhí Fú) 禽芮 (Qín Ruì) 杜门 (Dù Mén) Li 9 Wu/Xin Bing	螣蛇 (Téng Shé) 天柱 (Tiān Zhù) 景门 (Jǐng Mén) Kun 2 Gui Wu/Xin
九地 (Jiǔ Dì) 天辅 (Tiān Fǔ) 生门 (Shēng Mén) Zhen 3 Geng Ji	YangDun#2 Hour: BingShen ©Calvin Yap	太阴 (Tài Yīn) 天心 (Tiān Xīn) 死门 (Sǐ Mén) Dui 7 Ren Gui
玄武 (Xuán Wǔ) 马 天冲 (Tiān Chōng) 休门 (Xiū Mén) Gen 8 Ji Ding	白虎 (Bái Hǔ) 天任 (Tiān Rèn) 开门 (Kāi Mén) Kan 1 Ding Yi	六合 (Liù Hé) 天蓬 (Tiān Péng) 惊门 (Jīng Mén) Qian 6 Yi Ren

Michael Jordon home for 20+ years: 2700 Point Dr, Highland Park, IL 60035.

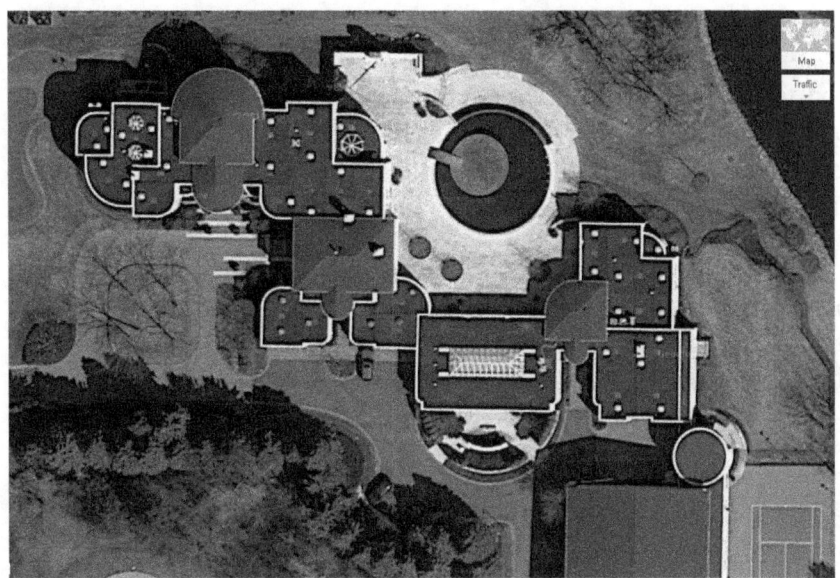

Source: Google Map

Sitting North, Facing South

YangDun#2 Hour: **BingShen** ; 直符(ZhíFú): **天禽(Tiān Qín)** ; 直使(ZhíShǐ): **死门 (Sǐ Mén)** ; 旬首(XúnShǒu): **JiaWuXin**		
九天 (Jiǔ Tiān) **O** 天英 (Tiān Yīng) 伤门 (Shāng Mén) Xun 4 Bing Geng	值符 (Zhí Fú) 禽芮 (Qín Ruì) 杜门 (Dù Mén) Li 9 Wu/Xin Bing	螣蛇 (Téng Shé) 天柱 (Tiān Zhù) 景门 (Jǐng Mén) Kun 2 Gui Wu/Xin
九地 (Jiǔ Dì) 天辅 (Tiān Fǔ) 生门 (Shēng Mén) Zhen 3 Geng Ji	YangDun#2 Hour: BingShen ©Calvin Yap	太阴 (Tài Yīn) 天心 (Tiān Xīn) 死门 (Sǐ Mén) Dui 7 Ren Gui
玄武 (Xuán Wǔ) 马 天冲 (Tiān Chōng) 休门 (Xiū Mén) Gen 8 Ji Ding	白虎 (Bái Hǔ) 天任 (Tiān Rèn) 开门 (Kāi Mén) Kan 1 Ding Yi	六合 (Liù Hé) 天蓬 (Tiān Péng) 惊门 (Jīng Mén) Qian 6 Yi Ren

In 1991, Jordan purchased a lot in Highland Park, Illinois, to build a 56,000 square foot mansion, which was completed four years later. This house was good for him. By mapping his bazi to the house's sitting which is Kan 1 Palace, there is 白虎 (Bái Hǔ) and 开门 (Kāi Mén). 开门 (Kāi Mén) is the Yong Shen (Useful God) for career and together with 白虎 (Bái Hǔ), his career would be a ferocious one.

Michael Jordon had gambling problem. During the Bulls' playoff run in 1993, controversy arose when Jordan was seen gambling in Atlantic City the night before a game against the New York Knicks. In that same year, he admitted to having to cover $57,000 in gambling losses and author Richard Esquinas wrote a book claiming he had won $1.25 million from Jordan on the golf course.

Yong Shen (Useful God) for gambling is 伤门 (Shāng Mén) which is at Xun 4 Palace but it is in Kong. Therefore, he didn't have gambling luck. However, he liked to gamble as 伤门 (Shāng Mén) is at Xun 4 Palace, which is Wood and it is in giving birth situation with his Day Master Xin at Li 9 Palace, which is Fire.

Case 25: Difficulties in conceiving

This was a case of a lady who had difficulties in conceiving. Both her kids died in her womb.

Her 1st child died in 1995 and her 2nd child died in 2002.

Date and time of birth: 20th March 1969 at 10:00

The chart is as follow:

Hour	Day	Month	Year
Ji	Jia	Ding	Ji
Si	Wu	Mao	You

YangDun#1 Hour: **JiSi** ; 直符(ZhíFú): **天蓬 (Tiān Péng)** ;
直使(ZhíShǐ): **休门 (Xiū Mén)** ; 旬首(XúnShǒu): **JiaZiWu**

九地 (Jiǔ Dì) 天柱 (Tiān Zhù) 景门 (Jǐng Mén) Xun 4 Ding Xin	九天 (Jiǔ Tiān) 天心 (Tiān Xīn) 死门 (Sǐ Mén) Li 9 Gui Yi	值符 (Zhí Fú) 天蓬 (Tiān Péng) 惊门 (Jīng Mén) Kun 2 Wu Ji/Ren
玄武 (Xuán Wǔ) 禽芮 (Qín Ruì) 杜门 (Dù Mén) Zhen 3 Ji/Ren Geng	YangDun#1 Hour: JiSi ©Calvin Yap	腾蛇 (Téng Shé) 天任 (Tiān Rèn) 开门 (Kāi Mén) Dui 7 Bing Ding
白虎 (Bái Hǔ) 天英 (Tiān Yīng) 伤门 (Shāng Mén) Gen 8 Yi Bing	六合 (Liù Hé) 天辅 (Tiān Fǔ) 生门 (Shēng Mén) Kan 1 Xin Wu	太阴 (Tài Yīn) O 马 天冲 (Tiān Chōng) 休门 (Xiū Mén) Qian 6 Geng Gui

Hour = children

Analysis

The Hour Heavenly Stem represents her children, which is Ji at Zhen 3 Palace. In that same palace, there is 杜门 (Dù Mén) and 天芮 (Tiān Ruì). 天芮 (Tiān Ruì) represents problem and 杜门 (Dù Mén) represent stuck. Therefore in her natal chart, she would have difficulties in conceiving.

1995 is Yi Hai year. Yi is at Gen 8 Palace and Hai is at Qian 6 Palace. Representing her child is Ji which is in Zhen 3 Palace. Zhen 3 Palace is in restricting relationship with Gen 8 Palace. Thus, the child is restricting Tai Sui Heavenly Stem Yi. Looking at Qian 6 Palace, it is also restricting Zhen 3 Palace. So, Tai Sui Earthly Branch Hai is restricting her child. As such, she lost her child that year.

2002 is Ren Wu year. Ren is at Zhen 3 Palace which is also her child palace. Wu is at Li 9 Palace with 九天 (Jiǔ Tiān) and 死门 (Sǐ Mén). Li 9 Palace is in giving birth situation with Zhen 3 Palace. However, 九天 (Jiǔ Tiān) and 死门 (Sǐ Mén) has the image of death and since it is in giving birth situation with Zhen 3. So, she lost her child that year.

World Cup Prediction Cases

Case 26: Brazil vs Croatia

This was the opening match for World Cup 2014. The match was playing at Sao Paulo on 12th June 2014 at 17:00

The chart is as follow:

Hour	Day	Month	Year
Gui	Jia	Geng	Jia
You	Yin	Wu	Wu

YangDun#3 Hour: **GuiYou** ; 直符(ZhíFú): **天冲 (Tiān Chōng)** ; 直使(ZhíShǐ): **伤门 (Shāng Mén)** ; 旬首(XúnShǒu): **JiaZiWu**		
太阴 (Tài Yīn) 天英 (Tiān Yīng) 杜门 (Dù Mén) Xun 4 Ding Ji	六合 (Liù Hé) 禽芮 (Qín Ruì) 景门 (Jǐng Mén) Li 9 Yi/Geng Ding	白虎 (Bái Hǔ) 天柱 (Tiān Zhù) 死门 (Sǐ Mén) Kun 2 Ren Yi/Geng
螣蛇 (Téng Shé) 天辅 (Tiān Fǔ) 伤门 (Shāng Mén) Zhen 3 Ji Wu	YangDun#3 Hour: GuiYou ©Calvin Yap	玄武 (Xuán Wǔ) 天心 (Tiān Xīn) 惊门 (Jīng Mén) Dui 7 Xin Ren
值符 (Zhí Fú) 天冲 (Tiān Chōng) 生门 (Shēng Mén) Gen 8 Wu Gui	九天 (Jiǔ Tiān) 天任 (Tiān Rèn) 休门 (Xiū Mén) Kan 1 Gui Bing	九地 (Jiǔ Dì) **O 马** 天蓬 (Tiān Péng) 开门 (Kāi Mén) Qian 6 Bing Xin

Analysis

For Qi Men Dun Jia soccer prediction, first we need to determine the Host and the Guest. In this case, Brazil is the host and Croatia is the guest. The Day Heavenly Stem represents the Host and the Hour Heavenly Stem represents the Guest.

In this chart, both Day and Hour heavenly stems are the same, which is Gui and is at Kan 1 Palace. In that palace, there is 九天 (Jiǔ Tiān), 天任 (Tiān Rèn) and 休门 (Xiū Mén). 休门 (Xiū Mén) and 九天 (Jiǔ Tiān) are considered auspicious so Host will win. Therefore, I predicted that Brazil would win.

Match result: Brazil won 3-1.

Case 27: Mexico vs Cameron

This was the 2nd match for World Cup 2014. The match was playing at Natal on 13th June 2014 at 13:00

The chart is as follow:

Hour	Day	Month	Year
Gui	Yi	Geng	Jia
Wei	Mao	Wu	Wu

YangDun#3 Hour: **GuiWei** ; 直符(ZhíFú): **天辅 (Tiān Fǔ)** ;
直使(ZhíShǐ): **杜门 (Dù Mén)** ; 旬首(XúnShǒu): **JiaXuJi**

太阴 (Tài Yīn) 马 禽芮 (Qín Ruì) 杜门 (Dù Mén) Xun 4 Yi/Geng Ji	六合 (Liù Hé) 天柱 (Tiān Zhù) 景门 (Jǐng Mén) Li 9 Ren Ding	白虎 (Bái Hǔ) O 天心 (Tiān Xīn) 死门 (Sǐ Mén) Kun 2 Xin Yi/Geng
螣蛇 (Téng Shé) 天英 (Tiān Yīng) 伤门 (Shāng Mén) Zhen 3 Ding Wu	YangDun#3 Hour: GuiWei ©Calvin Yap	玄武 (Xuán Wǔ) O 天蓬 (Tiān Péng) 惊门 (Jīng Mén) Dui 7 Bing Ren
值符 (Zhí Fú) 天辅 (Tiān Fǔ) 生门 (Shēng Mén) Gen 8 Ji Gui	九天 (Jiǔ Tiān) 天冲 (Tiān Chōng) 休门 (Xiū Mén) Kan 1 Wu Bing	九地 (Jiǔ Dì) 天任 (Tiān Rèn) 开门 (Kāi Mén) Qian 6 Gui Xin

Analysis

For Qi Men Dun Jia soccer prediction, we need to determine the Host and Guest. Comparing Natal, the place where the match was held, Cameron is nearer as compare to Mexico. As such, Cameron is the Host and Mexico is the Guest. In this case, Day Heavenly Stem Yi represents Cameron and Hour Heavenly Stem Gui is Mexico.

Day Heavenly Stem Yi is at Xun 4 Palace with 杜门 (Dù Mén), which means their goal keeper is good and is able to block away the goals. There is also a Horse star in the same palace. This also means that Cameron's players can run very well. However, there is 天芮 (Tiān Ruì), which means there is problem with the team.

Hour Heavenly Stem Gui is at Qian 6 Palace with 开门 (Kāi Mén), which means the goal is open and it's easy for opponent to score a goal. However, Qian 6 Palace is in restricting situation with Xun 4 Palace. As such, guest has higher chances of winning. Therefore, I predicted that Mexico would win.

Match result: Mexico won 1-0

Case 28: Spain vs Holland

This was the 3rd match for World Cup 2014. The match was playing at Salvador on 13th June 2014 at 16:00

The chart is as follow:

Hour	Day	Month	Year
Jia	Yi	Geng	Jia
Shen	Mao	Wu	Wu

YangDun#3 Hour: **JiaShen** ; 直符(ZhíFú): **天禽(Tiān Qín)** ;
直使(ZhíShǐ): **死门 (Sǐ Mén)** ; 旬首(XúnShǒu): **JiaShenGeng**

九地 (Jiǔ Dì) 天辅 (Tiān Fǔ) 杜门 (Dù Mén) Xun 4 Ji Ji	九天 (Jiǔ Tiān) O 天英 (Tiān Yīng) 景门 (Jǐng Mén) Li 9 Ding Ding	值符 (Zhí Fú) O 禽芮 (Qín Ruì) 死门 (Sǐ Mén) Kun 2 Yi/Geng Yi/Geng
玄武 (Xuán Wǔ) 天冲 (Tiān Chōng) 伤门 (Shāng Mén) Zhen 3 Wu Wu	YangDun#3 Hour: JiaShen **Fu Yin** ©Calvin Yap	螣蛇 (Téng Shé) 天柱 (Tiān Zhù) 惊门 (Jīng Mén) Dui 7 Ren Ren
白虎 (Bái Hǔ) 马 天任 (Tiān Rèn) 生门 (Shēng Mén) Gen 8 Gui Gui	六合 (Liù Hé) 天蓬 (Tiān Péng) 休门 (Xiū Mén) Kan 1 Bing Bing	太阴 (Tài Yīn) 天心 (Tiān Xīn) 开门 (Kāi Mén) Qian 6 Xin Xin

Analysis

For Qi Men Dun Jia soccer prediction, we will determine the Host and the Guest. The venue of the match was Salvador. Comparing the distance between Salvador and Spain vs Salvador and Holland, Spain is much nearer. As such, Spain is the Host while Holland is the Guest.

This is a Fu Yin chart. The Host is Day Heavenly Stem Yi which is at Kun 2 Palace will the Guest is Hour Heavenly Stem Geng which is also at Kun 2 Palace. In that same palace, there is 死门 (Sǐ Mén), which is bad. In addition there is 天芮 (Tiān Ruì), which represents problem. There is Kong in that palace.

Since both Hour and Day are on the same palace and the palace is bad, therefore I predicted that Guest which is Holland would win.

Match result: Holland won 5-1

Case 29: Chile vs Australia

This was the 4th match for World Cup 2014. The match was playing at Cuiaba on 13th June 2014 at 18:00

The chart is as follow:

Hour	Day	Month	Year
Yi	Yi	Geng	Jia
You	Mao	Wu	Wu

YangDun#3 Hour: **YiYou** ; 直符(ZhíFú): **天禽(Tiān Qín)** ;
直使(ZhíShǐ): **死门 (Sǐ Mén)** ; 旬首(XúnShǒu): **JiaShenGeng**

九地 (Jiǔ Dì) 天辅 (Tiān Fǔ) 生门 (Shēng Mén) Xun 4 Ji Ji	九天 (Jiǔ Tiān) O 天英 (Tiān Yīng) 伤门 (Shāng Mén) Li 9 Ding Ding	值符 (Zhí Fú) O 禽芮 (Qín Ruì) 杜门 (Dù Mén) Kun 2 Yi/Geng Yi/Geng
玄武 (Xuán Wǔ) 天冲 (Tiān Chōng) 休门 (Xiū Mén) Zhen 3 Wu Wu	YangDun#3 Hour: YiYou **Fu Yin** ©Calvin Yap	螣蛇 (Téng Shé) 天柱 (Tiān Zhù) 景门 (Jǐng Mén) Dui 7 Ren Ren
白虎 (Bái Hǔ) 天任 (Tiān Rèn) 开门 (Kāi Mén) Gen 8 Gui Gui	六合 (Liù Hé) 天蓬 (Tiān Péng) 惊门 (Jīng Mén) Kan 1 Bing Bing	太阴 (Tài Yīn) 马 天心 (Tiān Xīn) 死门 (Sǐ Mén) Qian 6 Xin Xin

Analysis

For Qi Men Dun Jia soccer prediction, we need to determine the Host and the Guest. The venue of the match was Cuiaba. Comparing the distance between Cuiaba and Chile vs Cuiaba and Australia, Chile is much nearer. As such, Chile is the Host while Australia is the Guest.

In this chart both the Hour and Day Heavenly Stem are the same, which is Yi at Kun 2 Palace. In that palace there is 杜门 (Dù Mén), which is auspicious for soccer prediction. In addition, there is 值符 (Zhí Fú), which represents referee. As such, since the palace is auspicious, therefore I predicted that the Host which is Chile would win.

Match result: Chile won 3-1.

Case 30: Columbia vs Greece

This was the 5th match for World Cup 2014. The match was playing at Belo Horizonte on 14th June 2014 at 13:00

The chart is as follow:

Hour	Day	Month	Year
Yi	Bing	Geng	Jia
Wei	Chen	Wu	Wu

YangDun#3 Hour: **YiWei** ; 直符(ZhíFú): **天心 (Tiān Xīn)** ;
直使(ZhíShǐ): **开门 (Kāi Mén)** ; 旬首(XúnShǒu): **JiaWuXin**

九地 (Jiǔ Dì) O 马 禽芮 (Qín Ruì) 景门 (Jǐng Mén) Xun 4 Yi/Geng Ji	九天 (Jiǔ Tiān) 天柱 (Tiān Zhù) 死门 (Sǐ Mén) Li 9 Ren Ding	值符 (Zhí Fú) 天心 (Tiān Xīn) 惊门 (Jīng Mén) Kun 2 Xin Yi/Geng
玄武 (Xuán Wǔ) 天英 (Tiān Yīng) 杜门 (Dù Mén) Zhen 3 Ding Wu	YangDun#3 Hour: YiWei ©Calvin Yap	螣蛇 (Téng Shé) 天蓬 (Tiān Péng) 开门 (Kāi Mén) Dui 7 Bing Ren
白虎 (Bái Hǔ) 天辅 (Tiān Fǔ) 伤门 (Shāng Mén) Gen 8 Ji Gui	六合 (Liù Hé) 天冲 (Tiān Chōng) 生门 (Shēng Mén) Kan 1 Wu Bing	太阴 (Tài Yīn) 天任 (Tiān Rèn) 休门 (Xiū Mén) Qian 6 Gui Xin

Analysis

For Qi Men Dun Jia soccer prediction, we will determine the Host and the Guest. The venue of the match was Belo Horizonte. Comparing the distance between Belo Horizonte and Columbia vs Belo Horizonte and Greece, Columbia is much nearer. As such Columbia is the Host and Greece is the Guest.

In this chart, Day Heavenly Stem Bing is at Dui 7 Palace with 开门 (Kāi Mén). That's mean the goal is open.

The Hour Heavenly Stem Yi is at Xun 4 Palace with 景门 (Jǐng Mén), 天芮 (Tiān Ruì) problem star and in Kong. This would mean the team has only 30% capability. In addition, the Hour Heavenly Stem Yi is at Xun 4 Palace which is Wood. The Day Heavenly Stem Bing is at Dui 7 Palace which is Metal. Metal restricts Wood. Hence, the Day Heavenly Stem restricts the Hour Heavenly Stem. Therefore, the Host restrict the Guest. As such, I predicted that the Host which is Columbia would win.

Match result: Columbia won 3-0.

Date Selection Cases

Case 31: Marina Bay Sands Opening
Background

Marina Bay Sands was open on 27th April 2010 at 15:18. On 12th June 2012, it was reported that a 46 years old male tourist fell to his death from the SkyPark, which is on top of the three hotel towers at Marina Bay Sands. It was said to be 200m above ground level.

On 21st June 2012, it was reported that another body had been found at the outdoor area of the Marina Bay Sands. The Straits Times reported that the body was found on Wednesday night near the Rise restaurant in the hotel lobby, located on the ground floor. The police arrived at MBS at about 9.05pm according to the account of a hotel guest.

The deceased was a 33-year-old man, who had entered Singapore on a tourist visa about a month ago and was staying in a suite on the 52nd floor of the hotel. The police had found $41,000 in the room and noted that the window was open. It was believed he may have fallen from the window into a courtyard next to the Rise restaurant on the ground floor.

Date and time of the opening ceremony: 27th April 2010 at 15:18

The chart is as follow:

Hour	Day	Month	Year
Wu	Ding	Geng	Geng
Shen	Wei	Chen	Yin

YangDun#8 Hour: **WuShen** ; 直符(ZhíFú): **天冲 (Tiān Chōng)** ; 直使(ZhíShǐ): **伤门 (Shāng Mén)** ; 旬首(XúnShǒu): **JiaChenRen**		
太阴 (Tài Yīn) 天英 (Tiān Yīng) 开门 (Kāi Mén) Xun 4 Ji Gui	六合 (Liù Hé) 禽芮 (Qín Ruì) 休门 (Xiū Mén) Li 9 Xin/Ding Ji	白虎 (Bái Hǔ) 天柱 (Tiān Zhù) 生门 (Shēng Mén) Kun 2 Yi Xin/Ding
螣蛇 (Téng Shé) O 天辅 (Tiān Fǔ) 惊门 (Jīng Mén) Zhen 3 Gui Ren	YangDun#8 Hour: WuShen ©Calvin Yap	玄武 (Xuán Wǔ) 天心 (Tiān Xīn) 伤门 (Shāng Mén) Dui 7 Bing Yi
值符 (Zhí Fú) O 马 天冲 (Tiān Chōng) 死门 (Sǐ Mén) Gen 8 Ren Wu	九天 (Jiǔ Tiān) 天任 (Tiān Rèn) 景门 (Jǐng Mén) Kan 1 Wu Geng	九地 (Jiǔ Dì) 天蓬 (Tiān Péng) 杜门 (Dù Mén) Qian 6 Geng Bing

Analysis

The Day Heavenly Stem Ding represents Marina Bay Sands. In this chart, it is at Li 9 Palace with 休门 (Xiū Mén), 天芮 (Tiān Ruì) and 六合 (Liù Hé). 休门 (Xiū Mén) means relax or place of relax. So, it suited Marina Bay Sands.

Wealth is represented by 生门 (Shēng Mén) which is at Kun 2 Palace with 白虎 (Bái Hǔ). 白虎 (Bái Hǔ) means ferocious and 生门 (Shēng Mén) means wealth. So, Marina Bay Sands is making money ferociously. The most important of all is that Kun 2 Palace is in giving birth situation with Li 9 Palace.

However, the hour chosen had its flaw. The Hour in this case is Wu which is at Kan 1 Palace with 景门 (Jǐng Mén) and 九天 (Jiǔ Tiān). 景门 (Jǐng Mén) represents blood related calamity. 九天 (Jiǔ Tiān) represents something high. So, it would mean there will be blood related calamity with someone falling from very high floor.

12th June 2012 before 15:00 chart is as follow:

Hour	Day	Month	Year
Xin	Jia	Bing	Ren
Wei	Chen	Wu	Chen

Mapping the incident date and time to the opening ceremony chart:

YangDun#8 Hour: **WuShen** ; 直符(ZhíFú): 天冲 **(Tiān Chōng)** ; 直使(ZhíShǐ): 伤门 **(Shāng Mén)** ; 旬首(XúnShǒu): **JiaChenRen**		
太阴 (Tài Yīn) 天英 (Tiān Yīng) 开门 (Kāi Mén) Xun 4 Ji Gui	六合 (Liù Hé) 禽芮 (Qín Ruì) 休门 (Xiū Mén) Li 9 Xin/Ding Ji	白虎 (Bái Hǔ) 天柱 (Tiān Zhù) 生门 (Shēng Mén) Kun 2 Yi Xin/Ding
螣蛇 (Téng Shé) O 天辅 (Tiān Fǔ) 惊门 (Jīng Mén) Zhen 3 Gui Ren	YangDun#8 Hour: WuShen ©Calvin Yap	玄武 (Xuán Wǔ) 天心 (Tiān Xīn) 伤门 (Shāng Mén) Dui 7 Bing Yi
值符 (Zhí Fú) O 马 天冲 (Tiān Chōng) 死门 (Sǐ Mén) Gen 8 Ren Wu	九天 (Jiǔ Tiān) 天任 (Tiān Rèn) 景门 (Jǐng Mén) Kan 1 Wu Geng	九地 (Jiǔ Dì) 天蓬 (Tiān Péng) 杜门 (Dù Mén) Qian 6 Geng Bing

2012 is Ren Chen Year. Ren is at Gen 8 Palace, which is originally in Kong and has only 20% capability but is now filled up. In Gen 8 Palace, there is 死门 (Sǐ Mén) which means there could be possibility of death. Chen is at Zhen 3 Palace which is in Kong but it is now fill up too. With 惊门 (Jīng Mén), it means there is shocking news. Besides, Gen 8 Palace is in restricts situation with Kan 1 Palace which represents the hour of the opening ceremony.

Bing Wu Month: We look at Li 9 Palace where Wu is residing. It has 六合 (Liù Hé) and 天芮 (Tiān Ruì) and it means relationship problem. At the same time, Li 9 is in restricts situation with Kan 1 Palace. Li 9 Palace represents Heart, so could be heart attack or head problem example mental problem.

Jia Chen Day: We will use Ren which happens to be at Gen 8 Palace as well. The Day Heavenly Stem Ren can also represent the tourist, with 死门 (Sǐ Mén), which means the person could be dead. Gen 8 Palace is also in restricts situation with Kan 1 Palace which is the hour of the opening ceremony.

Xin Wei Hour: Wei is at Kun 2 Palace and it is also in restricting situation with Kan 1 Palace which is the hour of the opening ceremony.

Kan 1 Palace is in restricting situation during the incident date and time. Kan 1 can also represent middle age (the tourist is 46 years old) and with 景门 (Jǐng Mén) and 九天 (Jiǔ Tiān) which represents blood calamity and high respectively. This could translate to blood calamity due to fall from high floor (SkyPark).

21st June 2012 at 21:05 chart is as follow:

Hour	Day	Month	Year
Ren	Gui	Bing	Ren
Xu	Chou	Wu	Chen

Mapping the incident date and time to the opening ceremony chart:

YangDun#8 Hour: **WuShen** ; 直符(ZhíFú): **天冲 (Tiān Chōng)** ; 直使(ZhíShǐ): **伤门 (Shāng Mén)** ; 旬首(XúnShǒu): **JiaChenRen**		
太阴 (Tài Yīn) 天英 (Tiān Yīng) 开门 (Kāi Mén) Xun 4 Ji Gui	六合 (Liù Hé) 禽芮 (Qín Ruì) 休门 (Xiū Mén) Li 9 Xin/Ding Ji	白虎 (Bái Hǔ) 天柱 (Tiān Zhù) 生门 (Shēng Mén) Kun 2 Yi Xin/Ding
螣蛇 (Téng Shé) O 天辅 (Tiān Fǔ) 惊门 (Jīng Mén) Zhen 3 Gui Ren	YangDun#8 Hour: WuShen ©Calvin Yap	玄武 (Xuán Wǔ) 天心 (Tiān Xīn) 伤门 (Shāng Mén) Dui 7 Bing Yi
值符 (Zhí Fú) O 马 天冲 (Tiān Chōng) 死门 (Sǐ Mén) Gen 8 Ren Wu	九天 (Jiǔ Tiān) 天任 (Tiān Rèn) 景门 (Jǐng Mén) Kan 1 Wu Geng	九地 (Jiǔ Dì) 天蓬 (Tiān Péng) 杜门 (Dù Mén) Qian 6 Geng Bing

Like the previous incident, all the indicators are at Gen 8 Palace and Zhen 3 Palace.

At Gen 8 Palace, there is Ren which is the Heavenly Stem for Year (Tai Sui) as well as the Hour of the incident that took place. Chen which is the (Tai Sui) Earthly Branch and it is at Zhen 3 Palace. Gui which is the Day Heavenly Stem of the incident is also at Zhen 3 Palace.

Case 32: Marriage date chosen ended in divorce

Background

This case was published in the fivearts forum (now defunct). A lady published her date of birth, her husband's date of birth and the date and time of her marriage. She also published her divorce year, which is in 1996. Both of them were born in the Geng year.

Date and time of the chart: 4th Sept 1983 at 15:00

The chart is as follow:

Hour	Day	Month	Year
Jia	Yi	Geng	Gui
Shen	Wei	Shen	Hai

YinDun#1 Hour: **JiaShen** ; 直符(ZhíFú): **天任 (Tiān Rèn)** ;
直使(ZhíShǐ): **生门 (Shēng Mén)** ; 旬首(XúnShǒu): **JiaShenGeng**

九地 (Jiǔ Dì) 天辅 (Tiān Fǔ) 杜门 (Dù Mén) Xun 4 Ding Ding	玄武 (Xuán Wǔ) O 天英 (Tiān Yīng) 景门 (Jǐng Mén) Li 9 Ji Ji	白虎 (Bái Hǔ) O 禽芮 (Qín Ruì) 死门 (Sǐ Mén) Kun 2 Yi/Gui Yi/Gui
九天 (Jiǔ Tiān) 天冲 (Tiān Chōng) 伤门 (Shāng Mén) Zhen 3 Bing Bing	YinDun#1 Hour: JiaShen **Fu Yin** ©Calvin Yap	六合 (Liù Hé) 天柱 (Tiān Zhù) 惊门 (Jīng Mén) Dui 7 Xin Xin
值符 (Zhí Fú) 马 天任 (Tiān Rèn) 生门 (Shēng Mén) Gen 8 Geng Geng	腾蛇 (Téng Shé) 天蓬 (Tiān Péng) 休门 (Xiū Mén) Kan 1 Wu Wu	太阴 (Tài Yīn) 天心 (Tiān Xīn) 开门 (Kāi Mén) Qian 6 Ren Ren

Analysis

This is a Fu Yin chart and using a Fu Yin chart to get married is definitely bad. Yong Shen (Useful God) for marriage is 六合 (Liù Hé) which is at Dui 7 Palace with 天柱 (Tiān Zhù) and 惊门 (Jīng Mén). 天柱 (Tiān Zhù) is a damaging star and together with 六合 (Liù Hé) means marriage will be damage. In addition, 惊门 (Jīng Mén) also means shock or sudden and therefore, the marriage will end up in shock or suddenly.

Both of them are born in the Geng year which is at Gen 8 Palace. Both of them are in external pan from 六合 (Liù Hé).

They divorced in 1996, which is a Bing Zi year. Bing is at Zhen 3 Palace which is clashing marriage Yong Shen 六合 (Liù Hé) at Dui 7 Palace. In addition, Zi is at Kan 1 Palace with 螣蛇 (Téng Shé) and 天蓬 (Tiān Péng). They are in giving birth situation with Dui 7 Palace. 天蓬 (Tiān Péng) means some one is here to steal the marriage.

Case 33: Singapore Flyer opening, ended with receivership

Background

The Singapore Flyer is a giant Ferris wheel in Singapore.

It is located beside Marina Bay Street Circuit, near the straight between turns 21 and 22 and the pit area. It affords great views of the Singapore Grand Prix. It also offers broad views of the city centre and beyond to about 45 km, including the Indonesian islands of Batam and Bintan, and Johor, Malaysia

In July 2008 the Flyer was stopped because of a minor fault in the braking system.

On 4 December 2008, the wheel was stuck for nearly five hours due to bad weather and some 70 people were stranded.

On 23 December 2008, the wheel stopped and trapped 173 passengers for about six hours. The breakdown was caused by a short circuit and fire in the Flyer's wheel control room, which cut off the air-conditioning in the wheel. Eleven passengers were evacuated via a sling-like device from a few of the capsules, and those stranded were given food and drink. The wheel started operating nearly seven hours after it had stopped and two people were hospitalized. The Flyer was closed indefinitely and an investigation into the cause of the malfunction was launched. The wheel re-opened on 26 January 2009 after the Singapore Police received the final safety certification report from the Conformity Assessment Board. Following this breakdown, additional back-up systems costing about S$3 million were installed. These included a generator, winches, three anti-fire and smoke systems, and heat detection devices.

On 18 July 2010, the ride was shut after one of its electrical cables supplying power to the air-conditioning systems was struck by lightning, affecting the air-conditioning system. Some 200 passengers had to be evacuated. The Flyer re-opened on 20 July 2010 after repair work was completed.

On 20 June 2013, operations were temporarily suspended to protect employees from record-high pollution levels in Singapore, the first time the Flyer had shut due to haze

On 28 May 2013, the Singapore Flyer announced that it was in receivership.

Date and time of the opening: 15ᵗʰ April 2008 at 20:00

The chart is as follow:

Hour	Day	Month	Year
Bing	Yi	Bing	Wu
Xu	You	Chen	Zi

YangDun#1 Hour: **BingXu** ; 直符(ZhíFú): **天冲 (Tiān Chōng)** ;
直使(ZhíShǐ): **伤门 (Shāng Mén)** ; 旬首(XúnShǒu): **JiaShenGeng**

太阴 (Tài Yīn) 天英 (Tiān Yīng) 休门 (Xiū Mén) Xun 4 Yi Xin	六合 (Liù Hé) O 禽芮 (Qín Ruì) 生门 (Shēng Mén) Li 9 Ji/Ren Yi	白虎 (Bái Hǔ) O 马 天柱 (Tiān Zhù) 伤门 (Shāng Mén) Kun 2 Ding Ji/Ren
螣蛇 (Téng Shé) 天辅 (Tiān Fǔ) 开门 (Kāi Mén) Zhen 3 Xin Geng	YangDun#1 Hour: BingXu ©Calvin Yap	玄武 (Xuán Wǔ) 天心 (Tiān Xīn) 杜门 (Dù Mén) Dui 7 Gui Ding
值符 (Zhí Fú) 天冲 (Tiān Chōng) 惊门 (Jīng Mén) Gen 8 Geng Bing	九天 (Jiǔ Tiān) 天任 (Tiān Rèn) 死门 (Sǐ Mén) Kan 1 Bing Wu	九地 (Jiǔ Dì) 天蓬 (Tiān Péng) 景门 (Jǐng Mén) Qian 6 Wu Gui

Analysis

The Hour Heavenly Stem Bing is at Kan 1 Palace with 九天 (Jiǔ Tiān) 天任 (Tiān Rèn) and 死门 (Sǐ Mén). 死门 (Sǐ Mén) is the worst Men among Ba Men in Qi Men Dun Jia. The Hour Heavenly Stem also represent the current matters and in this case, the opening of Singapore Flyer. 死门 (Sǐ Mén) represents dead. So, using this time for opening would mean death for Singapore Flyer.

Cash flow is represented by 生门 (Shēng Mén) which is at Li 9 Palace and is in Kong. That means there will be no profit. In addition, there is also 天芮 (Tiān Ruì) which represents problem. Therefore, Singapore Flyer could face cash flow problem.

If you notice, most of the problem happens in the month of July and December. July is where Kun 2 Palace is. In that palace, there is 白虎 (Bái Hǔ), 天柱 (Tiān Zhù) and 伤门 (Shāng Mén). 伤门 (Shāng Mén) represents transportation or engine. With 天柱 (Tiān Zhù) is a damaging star, hence, its means damage. 白虎 (Bái Hǔ) means ferocious. With combined analysis, we will have engine or mechanical problem.

December is where Kan 1 Palace is and it has 死门 (Sǐ Mén) in it. 死门 (Sǐ Mén) is bad, so problem usually happens during the month of Decemeber.

The End

Comments from Clients and Students

Post on Facebook on 5th Aug 2014:

Eowyn Jo

Calvin, thank you very much for your sharing. I am really glad that I've attended your QMDJ class. You've have made learning QMDJ so easy especially on date selection. I was really surprise when you presented the whole class with a tab. You had the date selection and chart plotting software loaded into the tab before giving it to us. This is really priceless!

Vin Leo

A selfless teacher shares all n thoughtful for the students. A selfish teacher makes you pay n offer no value in return.

From Facebook Message: 26th June 2014:

Thank you master, for the help, Hope I will get the job, I shall inform you about the result. Heaps of thanks once again for replying me soon.

Rao India.

Email from Thomas 11th Mar 2014:

From: Thomas <xxxx @hotmail.com>
To: Calvin Yap <calvin_yap@yahoo.com>
Sent: Tuesday, March 11, 2014 3:52 PM
Subject: RE: QMDJ course - questions

Hi Calvin,

I think the basic course is outstanding. I'm really glad to have studied it before moving to Bazi.

I think your course is very speciual and unique. It goes by far the deepest into divination.

Also the amount of case studies is very helpful to support the learning.

And the simplify system is really excellent, and your way to "get rid" of useless and confusing stuff that other people are teaching
and that you keep pointing to the essential parts of the method.

I appreciate a lot how you answer my questions. That's very helpful and a very important part of the course.

Thanks a lot & Best Regards,
Thomas.

Email from David 30th June 2013:

I greatly appreciate the time you have spent in assisting me, Thank You, Calvin

- David from US

Email from Mohan 9th August 2013

Hi, Thanks for your kindness. Thank you . Mohan.

-Mohan from India

Email from Jacqueline 8th Nov 2012

Calvin,

I don't think I can thank you enough for all your help. You've extended your help unselfishly and I appreciate all you have done. Not being in my home any longer is a blessing and I am much happier for it.

Thank you,
Jacqueline

Facebook Message: 4th Mar 2012:

Hi, fine! So I just purchased these 2 other books too. I am very happy to have you as my QMDJ teacher though the distance. I really appreciate your work, and already enjoy the reading of the Application book I started yesterday. It is clear and understandable and is a perfect starter before to go back to the oldest book.

Kind regards, Michael

Facebook Message: 23rd Feb 2012:

Hi,

I am from Poland and I am absolutely imressed by your book about Qi Men Dun Jia! I study this subject and I think it is extremely exciting! I have one your book and I will buy next - you are very good author! Thank you for sharing your knowledge. It will be honour for me to have you among my contacts!

Greetings from Poland!

Books from Author

Control Your Destiny by Mastering Qi Men Dun Jia

(ISBN: 978-981-08-7136-9)

This book is written in such a manner that it can be used as cover-to-cover reading, as well as for reference by practitioner. This book is divided into 5 parts: Part I – Basic, Part II – The Ingredient, Part III – Advanced Ingredient, Part IV – The cooking, Part V – the Fine Dining. So, it is similar to the process of preparing the food, cooking the food and eating the food.

This book begins by providing history of Qi Men Dun Jia and famous historic figures (e.g. Zhuge Liang, Mao Zedong) that used it to win war.

Part I - Basic is basic concept of Chinese Meta-Physics and it is for those who do not have any background in it. Understanding this section is important for those who want to, not only learn Qi Men Dun Jia but Chinese Meta-Physics as a whole.

Part II - The Ingredient breaks down each elements of Qi Men Dun Jia and its attributes.

Part III - Advanced Ingredient consists of more advanced information on Qi Men Dun Jia. It contains information about Stems Combinations, Ba Men combinations and Jiu Xing & Ba Men combinations. In addition, Qi Men Dun Jia special charts are provided and most importantly, it's usage.

Part IV - The Cooking, described how to plot Qi Men Dun Jia chart in 2 methods (Chai Bu and Zhi Run).

Part V - The Fine Dining is examples on how Qi Men Dun Jia can be applied.

Qi Men Dun Jia (奇门遁甲) Chāi Bù (拆布) English Calendar 2011 – 2020

(ISBN: 978-981-08-7386-8)

This book provides the Qi Men Dun Jia Chāi Bù (拆布) method charts and calendar in English. This will helps those who can't read Chinese to have access to Qi Men Dun Jia Chāi Bù (拆布) calendar. This book is organized into 3 parts.

The first part contains reference that you need to look for a Qi Men Dun Jia chart. The second part is Meta-physics calendar information from the year 2011 to 2020. This information allows you to plot the bazi for a given date and time as well as reference to the Qi Men Dun Jia Chāi Bù (拆布) 1080 charts. The third part contains all the Yang Dun and Yin Dun Qi Men Dun Jia Chāi Bù (拆布) chart.

By using the information in this book, you can easily obtain the appropriate Qi Men Dun Jia chart from a given date and time. You can then use the information from **Control Your Destiny by Mastering Qi Men Dun Jia** book for interpretation. In addition, based on your selection criteria, you can search the 1080 charts to look for an auspicious Qi Men Dun Jia chart. Then you can go to the calendar section to find a good date and time.

Practical Application of Qi Men Dun Jia (奇门遁甲)

(ISBN: 978-981-08-9837-3)

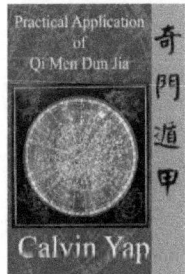

This book is written with lay person in mind. More than 80 Qi Men Dun Jia charts are used to illustrate the following:

Divination

- General Matters divination
- Marriage/Relationship
- Career
- Business Matter and Wealth Opportunity
- Products/Services
- Sickness
- Exam/Test/Study/Interview
- Fengshui condition of a house
- Finding empty parking lot or seat
- Accuracy of information

Application

- General Matters application
- Asking favor from boss
- Negotiation with boss
- Interview
- Proposal submission
- Business negotiation

Divination

For each type of divination, good and bad formations are being presented and explained in detailed. For example, for Marriage/Relationship, how to see problem in marriage, any 3rd party involve, who is rejecting who etc. For sickness, how to identify sickness and how to use the information to find a doctor that can help to cure the sickness.

Application

How to use the power of Qi Men Dun Jia to ask favor from boss, how to be successful in interview, proposal submission and business negotiation.

Qi Men Dun Jia Compendium Series

Volume 1: (ISBN: 978-981-07-0509-1)

Volume 2: (ISBN: 978-981-07-0510-7)

Volume 3: (ISBN: 978-981-07-0511-4)

The compendium series will provides comprehensive information available to readers that don't even exist in Chinese books.

Volume-1 consists of Qi Men Dun Jia Chāi Bù (拆布) and Zhí Rùn (直闰) Hour Qi Men method calendar in English from the year 1930 to 2020.

Volume-2 consists of Qi Men Dun Jia Yang Dun 540 charts with detail explanation of each chart by palace.

Volume-3 consists of Qi Men Dun Jia Yin Dun 540 charts with detail explanation of each chart by palace.

With the compendium series, readers can:
-Use the past event to plot the Qi Men Dun Jia chart and learn from past event
-Use the calendar to plot Qi Men Dun Jia chart based on birth date & time
-Instant interpretation of Qi Men Dun Jia chart from the information available at each palace
-Use the calendar and charts for Qi Men Dun Jia application (e.g. choosing a good date, time and location)
-Quick reference on auspicious and inauspicious Qi Men Dun Jia charts

Basic Qi Men Dun Jia - How to become a Fengshui Master

(ISBN: 978-981-071-745-2)

Authored by Master Ye Pei Ming
Translated by Calvin Yap

In 1985, Master Ye started learning Qi Men Dun Jia from an old man after a brief encounter in remote mountain of Guangxi. This old man has extraordinary skill in Yijing, Ba Gua and in particular Qi Men Dun Jia. Since then, he has been using the knowledge acquired on his job and day-to-day activities.

With the guidance from his master, he has further sharpened and simplifies the usage of Qi Men Dun Jia. In 2008, he published 2 Chinese books on Qi Men Dun Jia in Hong Kong. In his books, he revealed the secret techniques of simplified usage as well as techniques to remediate one's bazi using Qi Men Dun Jia Fengshui placements. Traditionally, such techniques will only be revealed discreetly but Master Ye decided to share it for the benefit of the general public. As such, he received a lot of gratitude messages from readers.

This book is part of the series that will help those readers that don't have knowledge of Qi Men Dun Jia, can quickly pickup and learn Qi Men Dun Jia. In particular, the usage of Qi Men Dun Jia 用神 (Useful God - yòng shén) and 5-element interaction.

This basic book is based on author's teaching experience and actual cases done. Readers can refer and practice based on the cases presented in this book to further sharpen your skill. After you have fully comprehended the techniques presented in this book, you will be able to use Qi Men Dun Jia to accertain what's really happening and further take control of the situation.

FengShui at Your Fingertips

(ISBN: 978-981-071-670-7)

In the past, we often saw ancient FengShui masters in movies deduce the FengShui formulas by tabulating their fingers. Now you can impress your clients by doing the same. This book will teach you how to memorized FengShui formulas by tabulating the fingertips. During my course of studying FengShui, I came in contact with various formulas. Sometimes these formulas need to be cross reference and it is time consuming to search and cross checked against each formula. As such, I start to research on quick and fast way to memorize the formulas. Ancient masters have 2 ways of memorizing the formulas; through poem and fingertips. I presented in this book, those formulas that can be easily memorized using the movement of fingertips. Formulas are:

- He Tu, Luo Shu & Ba Gua
- Combination and Clashes
- Heavenly Stems & Earthly Branches Combination, Clashes etc
- Shen Sha formulas (Hua Gai, Tao Hua, Jiang Xing etc)
- How to erect 4P without using a Calendar
- Flying Star & 8-Mansion
- How to find San Sha
- Qi Men Dun Jia

Note: This book will not explain why there is such and such formula, nor will it explain how these formulas to be applied. The purpose of this book is to help those studying Fengshui or Chinese Meta-Physics memorized the complex formulas.

Courses Available

Qi Men Dun Jia for day-to-day application

Availability: Classroom (Singapore only) & Distant Learning

Pre-requisite: Basic Chinese Meta-Physics concept (material will be provided FOC for those who don't have any background in Chinese Meta-Physics)

The class is divided into 2 parts:

- Basic Concept of Qi Men Dun Jia
- How to use Qi Men Dun Jia for day-to-day application.

At the end of the class you will know:

- Different categories of Chinese Meta-Physics
- What is Chinese Solar Calendar
- Basic Concept of Qi Men Dun Jia
- Using Master Ye simplify method of Qi Men Dun Jia to:
    - Forecast marriage & relationship
    - Forecast wealth and investment
    - Forecast interview and academic
    - Forecast prospect of investment
    - Forecast accuracy of information
    - Forecast on health

    - Forecast health and location for cure

Advanced QMDJ

Availability: Classroom (Singapore only) & Distant Learning

Pre-requisite: Basic QMDJ

At the end of the class you will know:

- Using Master Ye simplify method of Qi Men Dun Jia to:
    - Forecast on the Fengshui aspect of a house
- How to tap into the Heaven, Earth and Man Qi for:
    - Casino gambling
    - Horse racing
    - 4-D
    - Share Market prediction
    - Job interview and exam
    - Football prediction
    - Asking favour from boss
    - Negotiation

Note: we don't advocate gambling. The technique taught is for academic purpose only.

Bazi QMDJ

Pre-requisite: Basic QMDJ

At the end of the class you will know:

- How to use a person birth date/time to generate QMDJ chart
- How to derive the person:
    - Academic achievement
    - Career luck
    - Relationship luck
    - Direct Wealth luck
    - Indirect Wealth luck
    - Potential health issue
    - Character
    - Relationship of the person with his/her parents, siblings, spouse, offspring, marriage/relationship (3rd party etc)
    - Annual luck
    - Potential calamity

QMDJ Date Selection

Availability: Classroom (Singapore only) & Distant Learning

Pre-requisite: Qi Men Dun Jia for day-to-day application

The highest level of Qi Men Dun Jia is Date Selection. You will learn how read the outcome based on the date used for certain important events (e.g. the cause of marriage breakdown, health issue, company issues and financial difficulties because of wrong date used in move-in, ground breaking or marriage)

Real case studies are being presented on:

- Why certain date/time chosen will bring detrimental results
- How certain date/time chosen will bring good results.
- Learn how to choose a good date for specific outcome for:
- Renovation Date Selection
- Burial Date Selection
- Move-in Date Selection
- Opening ceremony Date Selection
- Marriage Date Selection
- Interview/Exam Date Selection
- Seek Wealth Date Selection

At the end of the class you will know:

- What are the criteria to look out for when choosing date/time for specific outcome
- How to derive what are the events going to happen when wrong date/time is chosen

Material:

- Course Material
- Software loaded on a tab to find a good date/time

Road to QMDJ Practitioner Program

This program is designed to prepare any serious students to become a successful QMDJ Practitioner. The objective of this program is to ensure that you have learnt and understood all the relevant techniques that are required to be a QMDJ Practitioner.

10 steps to become a practitioner:

1. Completed Qi Men Dun Jia for day-to-day application
2. Submission of 20 case studies based on the technique learnt in Qi Men Dun Jia for day-to-day application
3. Completed Bazi QMDJ
4. Submission of 20 case studies based on the technique learnt in Bazi QMDJ
5. Completed QMDJ Date Selection
6. Submission of 30 case studies based on the technique learnt in QMDJ Date Selection (from various categories)
7. Completed Advanced QMDJ
8. Interview session
9. Completed QMDJ Practitioner
10. Submission of 20 case studies

Each case submitted has to be from student's own case and not copying from other people's work. We will mark the submission and provide feedback. Correction has to be made if we deem that the technique used is not correct.

This program is a progressive program. You don't have to pay the full fee for the entire program. You only pay for the next course if you want to continue.

There is no time limit and you can take as long as you like to complete each individual course and the entire program.

After successfully completed the program, you will be presented with a medallion.

Products

Available online at: http://www.fengshui-hacks.com/

Qi Men Talismans

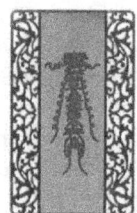

These talismans were invented by our grandmasters and only available through Master Ye. The creation of these talismans is based on special techniques used within Qi Men Dun Jia. The talisman can only be created on specific date/time and this can be achieved using Qi Men Dun Jia Date Selection. Based on specific date and time, the Qi Men Dun Jia "code" (i.e. Wealth, Study or Relationship) is embedded and locked into the Talisman. This is to ensure that the person using it will benefit from it. There are 3 types of Talisman available:

- Wealth
- Study
- Relationship

The Wealth Talisman is used to incease and retains wealth of the owner. The owner is advice to keep the Talisman inside his/her wallet.

The Study Talisman is for those who want to excel in their study or for those who require extra boost. This Talisman will help to get the support from 天辅 (Tiān Fŭ), the Study Useful God.

The Relationship Talisman is for those who want to maintain good relationship with their spouse or girlfriend/boyfriend.

---

5 Elephant on the Bridge

The **5-Elephant on the Bridge** is used to enhance relationship. This can be based on the annual prediction published by Master Ye so as to enhance relationship for that particular year. It can also be used to enhance individual relationship by displaying it in the house or room of individual. This requires analysis of bazi using Qi Men Dun Jia.

Maintain Wealth Horse

The **Maintain Wealth Horse** is used to sustain and increase the wealth of an individual. This horse is used as preventive measure to stop wealth from running away. This horse can be used based on the annual prediction published by Master Ye or can be used to prevent individual wealth from running away. For placement based on individual, bazi analysis using Qi Men Dun Jia is required.

Peaceful 3-Ram

The **Peaceful 3-Ram** has specific function annually. It is used to appease to the Annual Tai Sui. Based on the annual prediction published by Master Ye, the owner can place the **Peaceful 3-Ram** in the house to appease the Annual Tai Sui. For better accuracy, it is advice that proper consultation is done using the individual bazi so as to minimize the Tai Sui effect on individual. For example, if on that particular year, the person is offending the Tai Sui, your luck will not be smooth. There will be a lot of obstacle. Using the **Peaceful 3-Ram** will lighten the effect.

Golden Bull

The Golden Bull is used to help to increase an individual wealth. To use this **Golden Bull**, a detailed analysis of bazi using Qi Men Dun Jia is needed before it can be used effectively.

Qi Men home enhancement bronze elephant

The primary objective of this bronze elephant is to bring good fortune and wealth enhancement to your home. There are 2 variances to this bronze elephant. The one with trunk down is used to be placed at Wealth sector to "absorb" wealth (enhance wealth). The one with the trunk up is used to be placed at bad sector to "prevent" bad energy from manifesting. In addition, traditionally elephant is associated with luck and prosperity. Elephant is imposing but gentle. Elephant is good at absorbing water. Chinese regards water as wealth. If your house has window or balcony that faces water, you can put this bronze elephant to absorb wealth into your house.

This **Qi Men home enhancement bronze elephant** is designed based on special techniques that were passed down from previous Qi Men Dun Jia Masters. The major difference is that on both sides of this bronze elephant, there is Qi Men talisman imprinted on both side of the body. Different type of Qi Men talisman is used for different purposes. There is **Wealth Talisman** to bring in wealth, **Home Enhancement Talisman** for general home placement, **Career Talisman** for career opportunity, improve husband and wife **Relationship Talisman**, **Academic Talisman** to improve your study capability etc.

The Qi Men bronze elephant with the trunk facing down will absorb prosperous Qi and will enhance the sitting position. For example, in Fengshui study, it is advisable to have a mountain at sitting position (back) of the house. Elephant is a big animal and it is like a big mountain. Therefore, placing this Qi Men bronze elephant at the sitting position of living room, office or study, will increase the energy of the sitting position. In addition, it will increase your position as a leader (sitting position is regards as the position of a leader). Furthermore, the bronze elephant with the trunk facing down has the ability to absorb wealth from outside. Therefore, placing it facing a water features will increase the wealth of occupant, especially for those in business.

The Qi Men bronze elephant with the trunk facing up is like the elephant "blowing out" all the bad energy away. Together with the special Qi Men talisman and Qi Men 9-stars formation it can "blow away" all the bad Qi.

Chinese Character

Tradition vs Simplify Chinese

Traditionally, the Chinese characters are written in complex form which, through millions of years, transform from symbol that it represents. For example, the character horse:

Ancient character	Traditional Character	Simplify Character
	馬	马

Source: http://www.ancientscripts.com/chinese.html

After the formation of The People's Republic of China, a simplify form of writing Chinese character was adopted in China. In this book, the simplify Character is used.

Pinyin Representation:

Pinyin is a system for transliterating Chinese ideograms into the Roman alphabet, officially adopted by the People's Republic of China in 1979. The International Organization for Standardization adopted pinyin as the international standard in 1982. The system was adopted as the official standard in Taiwan in 2009, where it is generally referred to as the New Phonetic System.

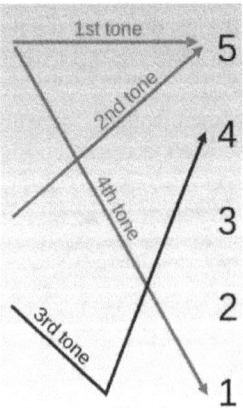

Chart showing the relative changes in pitch for the four tones of Mandarin Chinese. On a scale of 1 to 5 with 5 being the highest pitch, the first tone remains constant at 5, the second tone rises from 3 to 5, the third tone falls from 2 to 1 and then rises to 4, and the fourth tone falls from 5 to 1.

Information from Wereon (via Wikipedia)

Tones:
The first tone (Flat or High Level Tone) is represented by a macron (¯) added to the pinyin vowel:

ā ē ī ō ū

The second tone (Rising or High-Rising Tone) is denoted by an acute accent ('):

á é í ó ú

The third tone (Falling-Rising or Low Tone) is marked by a caron/háček (ˇ). It is not the rounded breve (˘), though a breve is sometimes substituted due to font limitations.

ă ĕ ĭ ŏ ŭ

The fourth tone (Falling or High-Falling Tone) is represented by a grave accent (`):

à è ì ò ù

The fifth tone (Neutral Tone) is represented by a normal vowel without any accent mark:

a e i o u

Characters used in Qi Men Dun Jia

Traditional Chinese Character	Simplify Chinese Character	Pinyin	[10]Explanation
八	八	Bā	Number 8
神	神	Shén	God
八神	八神	Bā Shén	8 Gods
值符	值符	Zhí Fú	Zhí means on-duty. Fú means a credential issued by ancient china. Zhí Fú means leader that is on-duty.
螣蛇	螣蛇	Téng Shé	Téng means winged. Shé means snake. Téng Shé means winged snake.
太陰	太阴	Tài Yīn	Tài means highest or greatest. Yīn means the opposite of Yang; darkness. Tài Yīn also means moon.
六合	六合	Liù Hé	Liù means 6. Hé means combine.
白虎	白虎	Bái Hǔ	Bái means white. Hǔ means tiger. Bái Hǔ means white tiger. White tiger is one of the 4 symbols of Chinese constellations.
玄武	玄武	Xuán Wǔ	Xuán Wǔ literally means The Dark Martiality or The Mysterious Martiality.
九地	九地	Jiǔ Dì	Jiǔ means 9. Dì means Earth, land or soil. Jiǔ Dì means 9 Earth or 9 land. Since 9 is the largest number in single digit numeral, Jiǔ Dì can also means something very small or short.
九天	九天	Jiǔ Tiān	Jiǔ means 9. Tiān means

---

[10] Some information extracted from http://www.zhongwen.com/

				Heaven or sky. Jiǔ Tiān means 9 Heaven and can also means something very grand, big or tall.
九星	九星	Jiǔ Xīng		Jiǔ means 9. Xīng means Star. Jiǔ Xīng = 9 stars.
天心	天心	Tiān Xīn		Tiān means Heaven. Xīn means Heart. Tiān Xīn means Heavenly Heart.
天蓬	天蓬	Tiān Péng		Tiān means Heaven. Péng is made up of 2 Chinese Characters: Flower (on top) + come upon (逢) =蓬 (twiggy leafy plant or promiscuous). Tiān Péng is also the name of a heavenly marshal. In the Journey to the West story, he was sent to earth after making some mistakes and later became the piggy (猪八戒 - zhū bā jiè). Tiān Péng means Heavenly Marshal.
天任	天任	Tiān Rèn		Tiān means Heaven. Rèn is made up of 2 Chinese Characters: People (人) + burden (壬) = people carrying the burden. Therefore, Rèn also means take up official post to serve the people. Tiān Rèn means Heavenly Post.
天冲	天冲	Tiān Chōng		Tiān means Heaven. Chōng is made up of 2 Chinese Characters: Water (水) + middle (中) = dilute. It also means rush, flush, dash, charge or clash. Tiān Chōng means Heavenly Clash.
天辅	天辅	Tiān Fǔ		Tiān means Heaven. Fǔ is made up of 2 Chinese Characters: Chariot (车) + Only (甫) = assist, complement or

			supplement. Tiān Fǔ means Heavenly Assistance.
天英	天英	Tiān Yīng	Tiān means Heaven. Yīng is made of 2 Chinese Characters: Flower on top of centre (央) = hero. Tiān Yīng means Heavenly Hero.
天禽	天禽	Tiān Qín	Tiān means Heaven. Qín means bird. Tiān Qín means Heavenly Bird.
天芮	天芮	Tiān Ruì	Tiān means Heaven. Ruì is made up of 2 Chinese Characters: Grass (on top) + inside (內). Ancient time when people are sick, they boil and drink herbs – putting grass inside the body. Therefore Ruì means sick or disease. Tiān Ruì means Heavenly Disease.
天柱	天柱	Tiān Zhù	Tiān means Heaven. Zhù is made up of 2 Chinese Characters: wood (木) + primary (主). Since it is a primary wood, it is a pillar. Tiān Zhù means Heavenly Pillar.
八門	八门	Bā Mén	Bā= 8. Mén = Door. Bā Mén means 8 doors.
開門	开门	Kāi Mén	Traditional writing of Kāi consists of the word Mén (門) with the character (开) inside. It is like a level for you to open the door. Therefore, Kāi means open.
休門	休门	Xiū Mén	Xiū is made up of 2 Chinese Characters: People (人) + tree (木). Normally people under the tree means to rest. Therefore, Xiū means rest.
生門	生门	Shēng Mén	Shēng is made up of 2 Chinese Characters: Plant rising from

				the ground (土). Therefore, Shēng means growth.
傷門	伤门		Shāng Mén	Shāng is made up of 2 Chinese Characters: People (人) with Yang (昜) or expose. Like an expose wound. Therefore, Shāng means hurt.
杜門	杜门		Dù Mén	Dù is made up of 2 Chinese Characters: tree (木) + earth (土) = stuck. Therefore, Dù means stuck.
景門	景门		Jǐng Mén	Jǐng is made up of 2 Chinese Characters: The Sun (日) over the capital (京) = scenery. Therefore, Jǐng means scenery.
死門	死门		Sǐ Mén	Sǐ is made up of 2 Chinese Characters: Evil (歹) + inverted person = dead. Therefore, Sǐ means dead.
惊門	惊门		Jīng Mén	Jīng is made up of 2 Chinese Characters: Heart radical + scenery = scare. Therefore, Jīng means scare.
甲	甲		Jiǎ	
乙	乙		Yǐ	
丙	丙		Bǐng	
丁	丁		Dīng	
戊	戊		Wù	
己	己		Jǐ	
庚	庚		Gēng	
辛	辛		Xīn	
壬	壬		Rén	
癸	癸		Guǐ	
子	子		Zi	
丑	丑		Chǒu	
寅	寅		Yín	
卯	卯		Mǎo	
辰	辰		Chén	
巳	巳		Sì	

午	午	Wǔ	
未	未	Wèi	
申	申	Shēn	
酉	酉	Yǒu	
戌	戌	Xū	
亥	亥	Hài	

Index

24 Sub-Season, 35
60 JiaZi, 35
8 God - Bā Shén, 38
9 Palaces, 27, 39, 41, 42
auspicious, 38, 39, 46
Ba Gua, 20, 23, 25, 26, 41
Bā Mén, 28, 42, 52, 61, 62, 63
bā shén, 28
Bā Shén, 38, 44
Bái Hǔ, 38
blood, 40, 43
business transaction, 43
calamity, 41, 43, 103
career, 43
Chāi Bù, 20, 52, 65
company, 43
documents, 43
Dun, 15, 26, 34, 44, 45, 46, 47, 51, 52, 54, 55, 56, 57, 58, 60, 61, 62, 63, 64, 65, 66
Earth, 20, 21, 25, 26, 27, 39, 40, 41, 42, 43
Earth Plate - dì pán, 41
Earthly Branches, 37, 41, 42, 64
Emptiness, 46, 64, 65
examination, 40, 43
External Pan, 48, 49
factory, 43
fengshui, 2, 12
Fire, 21, 25, 26, 27, 34, 40, 43
fú yín, 38, 44
Fú Yín, 44, 59, 60, 61, 62, 63
Heaven, 43
Heaven Plate, 39
Heaven, Earth & Man, 39, 41, 42, 43
Heavenly Stems, 34, 56, 57
Horse, 45, 65
Human Plate, 42
inauspicious, 38, 40, 43, 46

Internal Pan, 48, 49
Jiǔ Dì, 38
Jiǔ Tiān, 38
Jiǔ Xīng, 28, 39, 52, 60, 61
job, 43
Ju, 51, 52, 53, 54, 55, 56
judge, 43
Kōng, 46, 47, 64, 65
law suit, 43
lawsuit, 41
lawyer, 43
Liù Hé, 38, 44, 58, 59, 61, 64, 66, 206
Liu Yi, 34
management, 43
marriage, 45
martial art, 40
Metal, 21, 25, 26, 27, 34, 41, 43
plot, 51, 52, 55, 57
profit, 43
Qí Mén Dùn Jiǎ, 20
relationship, 34
San Qi, 34
scandal, 41, 43
Shāng Mén, 42, 43, 44, 61, 64, 66
shop front, 43
sickness, 27, 33
Tài Yīn, 38
teacher, 40
Téng Shé, 38
Tiān Chōng, 40
Tiān Fǔ, 39, 40, 44, 60, 61, 62, 64, 66
Tiān Péng, 40
Tiān Rèn, 40
Tiān Xīn, 39, 40, 44, 60, 61, 62, 64, 66
Tiān Zhù, 41
transportation, 43

Travelling, 65
Useful God, 33
Water, 21, 25, 26, 27, 43, 51
wealth, 43
Wood, 21, 25, 26, 27, 34, 40, 43
Xiū Mén, 42, 43, 44, 61, 64, 66
Xuán Wǔ, 38

Xún Shǒu, 47, 55, 57, 60
Yì Mǎ, 45, 65
Zhí Fú, 38, 44, 58, 59, 60, 61, 63, 64, 66
Zhí Rùn, 20
Zhūgě Liàng, 15, 94

www.ingramcontent.com/pod-product-compliance
Lightning Source LLC
Chambersburg PA
CBHW072236290426
44111CB00012B/2120